Henry M. (Henry Martyn) Field

Our western Archipelago

Henry M. (Henry Martyn) Field

Our western Archipelago

ISBN/EAN: 9783743320192

Manufactured in Europe, USA, Canada, Australia, Japa

Cover: Foto ©ninafisch / pixelio.de

Manufactured and distributed by brebook publishing software (www.brebook.com)

Henry M. (Henry Martyn) Field

Our western Archipelago

CONTENTS

CHAPTER I
THE LONGEST RAILROAD IN THE WORLD 1

CHAPTER II
ON THE NORTH SHORE OF LAKE SUPERIOR 15

CHAPTER III
IN RUPERT'S LAND—THE HUDSON BAY COMPANY . . . 25

CHAPTER IV
BANFF AND THE ROCKY MOUNTAIN PARK 35

CHAPTER V
HOW WE KEPT THE FOURTH OF JULY 44

CHAPTER VI
RIDING ON THE COW-CATCHER 55

CHAPTER VII
THE GLACIER OF THE SELKIRKS 65

CHAPTER VIII

To Vancouver and Victoria 76

CHAPTER IX

The Great American Archipelago 90

CHAPTER X

The Glaciers 103

CHAPTER XI

The Muir Glacier 108

CHAPTER XII

Nature and Man Farther North 117

CHAPTER XIII

Sitka and the Government 131

CHAPTER XIV

Schools and Missions 141

CHAPTER XV

The Story of Metlakahtla 151

CHAPTER XVI

Puget Sound—Seattle and Tacoma 161

CHAPTER XVII

The State of Washington 172

CONTENTS ix

CHAPTER XVIII

The City of Portland 179

CHAPTER XIX

Homeward Bound—The Strikes 189

CHAPTER XX

Montana—The Vigilantes 200

CHAPTER XXI

The Yellowstone Park 212

CHAPTER XXII

The Geysers 223

CHAPTER XXIII

The Lake and the River 230

CHAPTER XXIV

The Cañon of the Yellowstone 239

ILLUSTRATIONS

Mount Stephen with Field Station at the Foot	*Frontispiece*	
On the North Shore of Lake Superior	*To Face Page*	16
The Devil's Lake	" "	38
Kicking Horse Cañon	" "	58
Mount Field	" "	64
Bay of Chilcat	" "	106
Muir Glacier	" "	114
Mount St. Elias	" "	118
Bay of Sitka	" "	132
Mammoth Hot Springs	" "	216
Grand Cañon of the Yellowstone	" "	239
Falls of the Yellowstone	" "	246

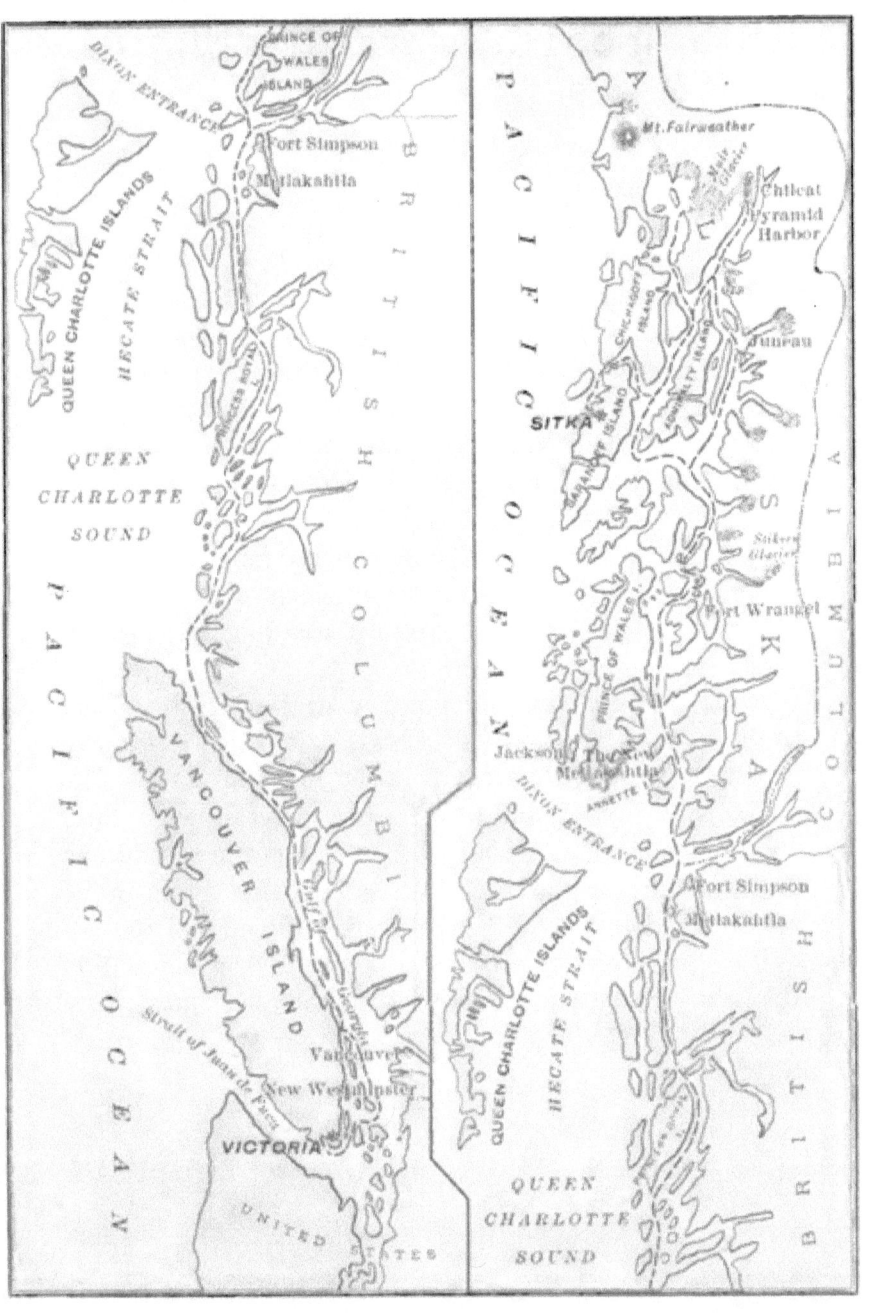

THE WESTERN ARCHIPELAGO

OUR WESTERN ARCHIPELAGO

CHAPTER I

THE LONGEST RAILROAD IN THE WORLD

When I was a boy it was a long way to Canada. I read the story of Arnold's Expedition to Quebec, and Quebec seemed as far away as Gibraltar. But we have changed all that, till it is a matter of but a few hours. We go to sleep in New York and open our eyes in Montreal. But it were a pity to flee away in the darkness; to "pass in the night" river and lake and mountain. Better choose the longest summer day for a ride along the banks of the Hudson and the shores of Lake Champlain, with the Green Mountains standing out against the horizon.

Montreal is a dear old place, dear because it *is* old. Coming from our new-built cities, it is a rest to the eye to look upon walls softened by the moss of time. The quaint old houses and the narrow streets, with their French names, make one feel as if he were in some town of Normandy; while the Cathedral, with its twin towers, recalls another Notre Dame on the banks of the Seine.

But just now my interest was not in the old but in the new. Since I was here before, no matter how many years ago, a tubular bridge had spanned the St. Lawrence, and a railway spanned the continent. I had come by invitation of the President of the Canadian Pacific, who had been a friend of my late brother Cyrus, and showed me kindness for his sake. Of course, my first duty was to acknowledge his courtesy. I found him in the great building erected for the use of the Company, where, with the walls covered with maps and photographs of wonderful scenery, he seemed to be standing in the very heart of the American Alps, through which the road winds its way—a road in which the Dominion of Canada has not only rivalled, but surpassed, the United States, inasmuch as, with its connections eastward to Nova Scotia, it is longer than any of our transcontinental lines, and is indeed the longest line of railroad under one management in the world!

In building on a scale so imperial we look for a certain proportion between the construction and constructors; so great a work should not be undertaken by weak men: hence it was with a sense of fitness that I recognized at once a strong personality in the man before me —a frame of iron, that could stand any pressure, and broad shoulders to carry heavy burdens, with a force of will to bear down all obstacles in his way. A man so compact with the elements of power looked as if he were the very embodiment of the energy needed to carry out so vast a design. Of course, with American inquisitiveness, I plied him with questions in regard to the enterprise to which he had given so large a portion of his life. Perhaps he answered the more freely in that he is himself one of our countrymen; but it is due to him to say that, while he entered into the narrative with the enthusiasm which had carried him through the work itself, he was very modest as to his own part in it, insisting that others had borne the burden and heat of the day. Of that we may form our own opinion hereafter. But for the present I will not detain my readers on the threshold of my story, stopping but a moment to tell how the Dominion came to build a highway from sea to sea.

Our own country led the way. For years a transcontinental railroad had been talked of, but rather vaguely, as a vast and almost Utopian enterprise; but the civil war showed it to be a political and military necessity. The war had awakened the country to a consciousness of its power. For four years it had been fighting for existence. That tremendous struggle was a revelation of the nation to itself. It had put great armies in the field; it had fought great battles and won great victories, out of which it came like a giant in his strength, to which there was nothing which it could not do or dare. To such unbounded energy a railroad to the Pacific did not seem impossible. It was only necessary to put a little of the spirit shown in war into the work of peace. And as to the cost, a country that had been accustomed to spend five millions a day, need not shrink from lending its credit to an enterprise which would bind together the Union which had cost so much in treasure and in blood. Hence the enormous subsidies in public lands and government bonds, to build the first railroad across the American Continent.

The lesson of all this was not lost upon our neighbors over the border. Our war had consolidated the Union, while British America remained divided into half a dozen provinces: on the east, Newfoundland, Nova Scotia, and New Brunswick; then Upper and Lower Canada; and in the far west, British Columbia; besides the vast, undefined territories under the control of the Hudson Bay Company, which, like the East India Company, had grown from being a commercial corporation to become a great political power, whose rule stretched westward almost to the Pacific, and northward to the Arctic Circle. Not only were all these divisions of the British possessions distinct from one another, but in some cases they were farther separated by rival interests and mutual jealousies. To eliminate these sources of weakness and danger, it was proposed to combine all these provinces into one confederation, after the manner of the United States.

The design was worthy of great statesmen. But it was not so easy to carry it out, for however small a province may be, and however petty its government, it does not like to be swallowed up in a great coalition, in which it will sink into insignificance. At any rate, if it consents to self-annihilation, it must have some very substantial consideration, and such was offered in the promise of a line of railway that should span the continent, and thus bind all the provinces together.

But great bodies move slowly, and although the project was first mooted in 1867, the work was not begun until 1875, when it was undertaken by the Government with all the stately dignity that belongs to Government operations. To be sure, this patronage gave it unbounded credit. Books had but to be opened in the great financial centres to call out large subscriptions. With such resources the Government carried on the work for five or six years, in which it built nearly six hundred miles. By this time it had come to appreciate the enormous difficulties to be overcome. The obstacles seemed to increase at every step, and bid fair to exhaust the strength, great as it was, of the Government itself, which at last staggered under the tremendous load, and the work stood still!

Then came into the field a new element—that of individual enterprise, which dared to undertake what a more showy but more cumbrous machinery had failed to achieve. The Government was generous to its successor, to which it turned over all it had done, and besides gave outright twenty-five millions of dollars and twenty-five millions of acres of land along the road, a liberality which it owed chiefly to the Prime Minister, Sir John A. Macdonald, who may be called the Father of the Canadian Pacific.

With this magnificent subsidy the new Company started on its way, in 1881, full of courage and of hope. It was fortunate in finding a very efficient General Manager in one of our own countrymen, a native of Illinois—a State that grows strong men as well as great harvests—who had been trained on our Western railways, where he had made himself so familiar with every detail that he became one of the first masters of railroad construction in the country, understanding its whole art and mystery, so that he knew how to build an engine as well as any machinist, and to run a locomotive as well as any engineer—a practical discipline which prepared him for larger responsibilities, when he was invited to cross the border from the Great Republic to the Dominion of Canada. He took charge of the work in the field, and pressed it forward with the greatest vigor. For part of the distance it was easy enough. From Winnipeg westward the country is a plain for a thousand miles. Here was nothing to check their progress, and they swept on, carrying everything before them, sometimes laying down the track at the rate of five, and even seven, miles a day. But the great obstacles lay at the two ends east and west—on the rock-bound shore of Lake Superior, and near the Pacific Coast, where it had to traverse three distinct ranges of mountains—the Rockies, the Selkirks, and the Cascades; so that literally Alps on Alps arose to bar the passage to the sea.

But the immensity of the undertaking only stimulated their courage. As fast as the work was done in one section, the corps of engineers that had gone in advance led the way to another, pointing out the track to be laid, the bridges to be built, and the tunnels to be cut through the mountains, which the miners attacked with powder and dynamite for blasting the rocks, and cutting passages through the bowels of the earth.

The eagerness to press forward was the greater because they were running a race with a competitor on the other side of the border. It was the Canadian Pacific against the Northern Pacific, which had the start, and was farther on its way. But still they were parallel lines, between which there was a generous rivalship, which increased as the latter was advancing with rapid strides towards completion. It was not long before it was carried through, and opened to the public with a grand demonstration in which orators brought from the East celebrated the enterprise, the wealth, and the power of the Great Republic!

But alas for all human glory! In one hour was so great riches brought to naught. The road was indeed complete, but at such enormous cost that the Company was nearly bankrupted, and the sudden collapse almost produced a panic in the country. I have occasion to remember it, as I knew some of the sufferers, among whom was the late Frederick Billings, who had devoted his fortune and his life to this great enterprise. In the very midst of the panic I spent an evening at his house. Of course, my first question was "How he felt in these troublous times?" to which he answered with his wonted composure, "As well as a man can who is losing a hundred thousand dollars a day!" Fortunately, he could bear the loss with an equanimity which others could not assume who were wrecked and ruined.

The effect on the Canadian Company was instantaneous—to discredit any and every attempt to build a trans-continental railway; for, if a road that was done and in full operation could not even pay the interest on its bonds, what was to be expected from one that was not yet finished, and on which there were still millions to expend?

It was in this extremity—of all times in the world— that they turned once more to the Government for help. They had nowhere else to go. The bottom had dropped out. As to the credit of the Company, it had no credit, for confidence was utterly destroyed. The banks would not lend it a dollar, and pressed it for loans already given. As my informant described it, the "interest fiend" was after them like a pack of wolves, whose cry came nearer and nearer. It was at such a moment that the Company came to the Government to stand between them and death. They did not indeed ask for another bonus, a gift outright, (that would have been too much), but for a loan of thirty millions! At this modest request the officers of the Government shook their heads. They thought they had done enough, and some even went so far as to say that they had rather lose the twenty-five million dollars they had already advanced than to put in any more! If, with all the help it had received, the

Company could not take care of itself, they would leave it to its fate.

This was a very natural feeling, and yet it was met by a very effective answer: "The Government *could not* throw the Company overboard without sharing in its humiliation, and discrediting itself. In the United States the failure of certain enterprises in 1873 had created a panic, and caused a depression that spread over the country and lasted four years, in which were lost untold millions. Did the Dominion intend to follow in the same course, and inflict a loss many times greater than all that it was now asked to guarantee?" This reasoning prevailed, and at last the Government put its official seal on the new loan, which restored the credit of the Company, so that it could once more look the world in the face, and take heart again to complete its magnificent design. But while it worked on, and worked for dear life, it had the terror of failure always hanging over it, and sometimes had to take courage from despair. Those were the days of darkness, and they were many. At last it became a race between life and death; they lived by the day; not knowing but the morrow would close their career, and end their work in ignominy and disgrace. When such was the state of things, it required no small self-control to hide the dreadful secret. "But," so ran the story, "we never told anybody in what straits we were, but put on a bold front, and tried to keep up a stout heart, though sometimes those about us would have been dumbfounded if they knew in what extremities we were. There were times when we had hardly a dollar in the treasury, and yet were spending a hundred thousand dollars a day! At one time it was a question of hours how long we could keep afloat. One day we had to make a payment of four hundred thousand dollars. If it had not been paid by three o'clock the Company's paper would have been protested, and it was near noon before we knew that we could get the money!" Such hairbreadth escapes are very thrilling to tell of, but at the moment of experience they are like the crisis of a battle. But it is these very crises that try men's souls, and show of what stuff they are made. A battle is hardest, not at the beginning, but at the end, when, if courage is not gone, strength is nearly exhausted. As Napoleon said, "It is those who keep on fighting till two o'clock in the morning who win the day!" Never was more of such courage shown than by the projectors and constructors of the Canadian Pacific Railway. The story of their struggles is as thrilling as that of a military campaign, with marches, sieges, and battles. Indeed, it was one long battle, with frequent repulses and seeming defeats, which would have been real defeats but that it could be said of them, as has been said of British soldiers, that they never knew when they were beaten, and kept on fighting till at last the tide turned in their favor, and the victory was won. And what a victory! They had ten years to do their work—they did it in five!

But there was something better still to wind up this great achievement. When the Company pleaded for its life, to obtain its last loan, probably not a man in the Government expected ever to see the money again. What was called by courtesy a loan would be really a gift. But to the honor of the Company be it said, that within a year after the road was completed and running, every dollar of the thirty millions—principal and interest—was paid back again!

"And to whom do you ascribe the honor of this great success?" I asked.

"First of all, to Sir John A. Macdonald, who was the most prominent in its inception, who believed in it from the beginning, and stood by it to the end. The Dominion of Canada owes him a debt which it can never repay, a debt which should be recognized more than ever now that he is gone to the grave.

"The glory of carrying out the work belongs to two Scotchmen, now honored by the Home Government as Lord Mount Stephen and Sir Donald A. Smith, who may be almost said, like the signers of the Declaration of Independence, to have 'pledged to it their lives, their fortunes, and their sacred honor.' Lord Mount Stephen was the financier and the master mind in the execution of the great design; and Sir Donald was his strong and unfailing prop. Nobody else can be mentioned on the same page, unless it be Richard B. Angus, one of the original syndicate, who, with Lord Mount Stephen and Sir Donald, saw the enterprise through to the end."

I had my own opinion that there was another figure that was very conspicuous in this March to the Sea, but my informant put himself in the background, saying, "My own part was that of spending money, not always wisely, I fear, but at best an insignificant one as compared with the others."

But if he is so modest as to decline the honors, he must at least permit his own countrymen, who feel a national pride in what he has done on the other side of the border, to do him justice. As I learn more of the history of the Canadian Pacific, not from him only, but from others, it seems to me that he was just the man for the crisis. One could not talk with him, as I did, for an hour or two, without seeing that he had an extraordinary quickness of perception, and a power of statement that made others see things as he saw them. Even I, outsider as I was, and ignorant of such matters as a man of books is apt to be, began to see a little into the magnitude of the work and the greatness of the man. Such a man inspires confidence in his judgment, and infuses into others a portion of his own indomitable spirit, so that they are ready to follow where he leads the way. He had to take great responsibilities. An industrial force composed of thousands of men is an army, and can only be made efficient by a sort of military discipline, that requires a military genius; that is, a genius for organization and for leadership, in both which I have seen few men so masterful. Not only did he take in every situation at a glance, and see the thing to be done, and done on the instant, but he had a restless activity, which enabled him to be in a dozen places at once, guiding, directing, and inspiring—keeping his army well in hand, filling up the ranks and pushing on the reserves, so that there should be no false movement, and no wasted labor. These are the qualities of a great commander, a proud title, but one to which few men have so just a claim.

That I am not alone in my estimate of the value of his services is shown by the fact that they have been fully recognized by the Government. Republics may be ungrateful, but royalties are not so forgetful, with whom it is among the traditions of honor to remember by some title or tribute those who have rendered services to the State, whether victories in war, or achievements in peace; and the fact that our countryman is now Sir William C. Van Horne, President of the Canadian Pacific, is the best proof of the way in which he is regarded in the Dominion that he has served so well. And we may add, not one country only, for a railway that spans a continent and unites two oceans, and so brings Western Europe nearer to Eastern Asia, is a service to civilization, as it is a means of promoting the friendly intercourse of mankind.

But delightful as it was to listen to one who had done so much to make history, our interview had to come to an end, for we had the long journey across the continent before us, and on the second day in the afternoon we turned westward.

A few hours brought us to Ottawa, the capital of the Dominion of Canada, where Parliament was now in session; and though it was ten o'clock at night, we saw the Parliament House lighted up across the river, (for it stands on a river, as the Parliament House in London stands on the Thames). It is a noble pile, even if we cannot quite agree with the Canadians in thinking it almost equal to the grander pile that stands opposite Westminster Abbey. As I had an order of admission from the Speaker, we were shown into his private gallery, from which we looked down upon the House of Commons, and saw the Prime Minister, Sir John Thompson, sitting at the head of the Treasury Bench. I met him last year in Paris, where he was one of the British commissioners on the Bering Sea Arbitration; and though my acquaintance was of the slightest, he had then received me so cordially that I ventured to send him my card. He came out immediately and gave us a hearty welcome, and took us into his private room, and talked of Canadian politics (there had just been an election in the great Province of Ontario, which had gone against him) without any show of partisan feeling. Men of all parties concede that he is a man of very great ability, as well as devotion to the interests of the country. Canada is fortunate in having such a Prime Minister, and at the same time having Lord Aberdeen, the intimate and trusted friend of Mr. Gladstone, as its Governor-General. He is one of the purest and best of the public men of England, while Lady Aberdeen is the leader in all charities. Such examples in high station are worth everything to the good government and official life of Canada.

Sir John Thompson spoke of the relations of England and America, with the greatest satisfaction that every cause of irritation between the two countries had been removed by the Bering Sea Arbitration; and as for Canada and the United States, as they were the nearest neighbors, they should remain forever the closest friends.

This brief interview I recall with the greater interest, that, within a few months after, one whose future was so full of promise came to the end of his career. No Englishman this side of the Atlantic was more trusted by the Home Government, by which he was made a member of the Privy Council, and summoned to London to receive the great honor, and with the ministers went to Windsor Castle to be presented to the Queen, where he was suddenly stricken with death. The event created a great sensation in England as well as in Canada. A ship of war brought his remains to Halifax, where he was laid to rest, with a military display such as has seldom been witnessed. He was only in his fiftieth year.

As we parted, he expressed great regret that I could not remain till the next day, when there was to be a meeting of colonial delegates from all parts of the world

—from Melbourne and Sydney and South Africa, even from the Dutch State nearest the Cape of Good Hope, etc., to see if they could not combine in efforts to promote their freer mutual intercourse, and their common good, by increased means of communication, subsidizing new lines of ships, and laying submarine telegraphs to the Sandwich Islands and to the great ports of Australia and New Zealand. This would be a first step towards

"A parliament of nations, the federation of the world."

With such a picture of the good time coming, it was hard not to be able to wait over one day to see the dawning of the millennium. But even the prophecy, if it were only a beautiful dream, was a vision that shone in the distance, like the lights in the Parliament House, as we sailed away into the silence and darkness of the night.

CHAPTER II

ON THE NORTH SHORE OF LAKE SUPERIOR

To wake up in a sleeper on a train bound for the Pacific is like waking up at sea. We have lost our bearings and hardly know the points of compass. But we rub our eyes, and, when we are sufficiently awake to take our latitude and longitude, find that we are not in mid-ocean but in mid-Ontario, in the heart of what used to be called Upper Canada—a territory that is almost as boundless as the sea, and as lonely also in the gloom of its forests. Even in its more settled portions, towns and villages do not crowd on each other here as in New England, while cities are few and far between; so that the general impression of the country, as one rides over it, is of magnificent distances, rather than of a dense population. Still the land is cultivated, and the settlements along the road are alive with the hum of industry. The sawmills are as frequent an object in the landscape as windmills in Holland, and around them are piles of lumber and booms of logs that have been floated down the rivers. This is an industry that is grateful to more senses than one; the sound of the buzzing of the saw is not unmusical to the ear, while the traveller inhales with delight the sweet odor of the pines. The forests of Canada are said to be inexhaustible. It is a fact of cheer to us, as we see the forests of Michigan and Wisconsin falling before the axe, to know that on the other side of the border there is a supply that will last for generations to come.

As a railroad centre, the chief point of interest is Sudbury, where we come to the parting of the ways or, rather, are overtaken by another train from Montreal, called the "Soo Express," which is bound to the southwest, along the shore of Lake Huron, till, at a distance of one hundred and seventy-nine miles, it strikes the "Soo" (the Sault Ste. Marie), the outlet of Lake Superior, that is spanned by an enormous iron bridge, over which the train passes into "the States," careering through Wisconsin into Minnesota, and from St. Paul turning again (like a lost child that has strayed away from its mother) to the northwest; and, after another long stretch through North Dakota, reëntering the Dominion, far away in Assiniboia, where it joins the trunk line of the Canadian Pacific.

But, inviting as this route might be, we who were bound straight for Alaska kept to the train in which we were embarked, and bore away still farther to the north, around the shore of Lake Superior, the largest body of fresh water on the globe, with a coast-line worthy of its greatness.

To the wandering Scot it seems as if he were in the stormy Hebrides, in the Sound of Mull, as he looks at the great basaltic columns standing out of the water and in the water, while the railway, darting in and out of innumerable tunnels, reminds one of the course along the Riviera, at the foot of the Maritime Alps, which bend their heads and stoop so proudly to the Mediterranean, compelling those who would find a way between the mountains and the sea to force a passage through the

ON THE NORTH SHORE OF LAKE SUPERIOR.

solid rock. Here the subterranean plunge is repeated, though against far greater obstacles. There are rocks and rocks. Some are so friable that they almost crumble to the touch or are broken in pieces by the slightest explosion of gunpowder, while others yield only to heavy charges of dynamite; and nothing in the spurs of the Alps had such a power of resistance as the cliffs of basalt on the northern shore of Lake Superior, of which it is not enough to say that it is rock-bound, for it is iron-bound, requiring the utmost skill of man to break through it or to batter it down. This was the hardest nut to crack in the construction of the Canadian railway across the continent—an obstacle more formidable even than the triple range of mountains on the Pacific coast.

Nor is this iron-bound shore without its historical associations, as we find in touching at Port Arthur and Fort William, with its Thunder Bay, old stations of the Hudson Bay Company.

At last we leave the lake behind and bear away into the interior, through interminable woods, which, however, are not very grand, as they have been in many places burnt over, leaving but charred trunks that look like spooks, if you should happen to pass through them in the moonlight. But in the daytime this sombre landscape is relieved by hundreds of small lakes, which are so still that they seem to be scattered along the dark forest-road only to reflect the fleecy clouds that are sailing across the sky.

As we push westward, the country rises gently, till it reaches an altitude of twelve hundred feet above the level of the sea, at which the waters divide, those on the one side flowing into the Lakes, while those on the other turn towards the Pole, the rivulets trickling into streams, till the streams are swollen into rivers, that take their long and winding course (but in one general direction, as if following the North Star), till they find rest in the waters of Hudson Bay.

At this high level and high latitude—for we are on the fiftieth parallel—the cold is at the extreme; the winters are long, and the mercury drops down, down, till not unfrequently it touches forty degrees below zero, and freezes in the bulb! At this temperature it might seem that life could hardly exist, and yet the realm of frost and snow has its own life; which, perchance, is not less full of pleasure than ours. Man cannot slumber at noontide as in tropical climes. The sharp frost pricks him to wakefulness, and he finds his keenest delight in intense activity. With the jingle of sleigh bells, one might, now and then, give himself, by way of variety, the pleasure of a ride with a team of dogs. These are for the most part left to the Indians, or half-breeds, who come from the North in sledges laden with furs. But in these days, when horses are exchanged for bicycles, it might be an agreeable revival of the old times if visitors from abroad could be entertained with a ride in the real old Esquimaux fashion. Dogs can go where horses cannot; where the heavy hoofs, shod with iron, would break through the crusted snow, it may be hard enough to bear up the weight of a lighter beast of burden, whose shaggy covering protects him from the cold, while his soft foot rests on the snow as that of the camel rests on the sand of the desert. A stout dog will draw a hundred pounds' weight all day long; and a full team will set things flying. We saw many fine specimens round the stations, where they keep watch for the coming of the trains and, with unerring instinct, make for the car which sends forth a savory smell, as the cook is preparing dinner; and a niggardly fellow he must be if he does not reserve some bits of meat for these faithful attendants, who stick to him closer than a brother. He may think them lazy pensioners on his bounty, but let him wait till winter comes, and they will pay for their keep by heroic duty, when these petted household companions are harnessed for a service which only they can perform. The woodman himself is proof against the elements when he can wrap himself in furs that thoughtful nature has provided for this arctic climate, and there is a thrill in his veins as he speeds over the smooth surface with a swiftness like that of the wind itself. Those who make a study of pleasure tell us of the exhilaration of tobogganing, but this is tame compared to that of being harnessed to a team of Esquimaux dogs and flying in the face of the keen and frosty air over the untrodden snow.

As the long stretch is somewhat monotonous, we turn to books, or to fellow-travellers with whom we may be thrown in company. The first morning after we left Ottawa I had observed an old gentleman sitting apart, and turning to him as one who might give me information, I asked if he knew anything about the country, or was, like myself, a stranger. "Oh, yes," he said; "I know it well, for I was born here!" This took me aback, for he had already told me that he was seventy-two years old; and seventy-two years ago I thought there was no white inhabitant in the country, or any way of getting up the St. Lawrence. But this reminded me that Winnipeg, instead of being a new settlement, is an old one, much older than most of the towns and cities of the United States. How his father came to be here, was an interesting story. In the first decade of this century, when England was fighting against Napoleon, a young Scotchman by the name of Sutherland enlisted in the army that fought under Sir John Moore in Portugal, and was with him when he fell at Corunna, after which Wellington took command, whom the young infantryman followed in all his campaigns from Portugal into Spain, and across it, till they passed the Pyrenees and were on the soil of France, and so on and on till 1814, when Napoleon abdicated and retired to Elba. Then, thinking that all was over, he was mustered out of service and returned to his native Scotland. But what was there for an old soldier to do amid the peaceful scenes of the Scottish Highlands? They had not changed, but he had changed; "grim-visaged war" had left in him little of the ploughman; and, like many of his companions in arms, he turned his eyes across the sea, and there determined to make his home. He had taken his passage, and gone on board, when came the astounding report that Napoleon had escaped from Elba and the war was to begin again! "Had the news come in the morning," the old man was wont to say in after years, "I should have left the ship and gone back and taken my place in the ranks." Perhaps he might have fallen at Waterloo. But the hour was late, night was coming on, and he decided to commit himself to the waves. In those days it was a long passage across the sea. But after many weeks he entered the strait that leads to Hudson Bay, and crossing the country by the Indian trail, and the portage familiar to trappers and traders, at last reached Winnipeg, where the old soldier found a good Scotchwoman who was willing to share his humble fortunes, and they had sons and daughters born to them. And that this venture in the New World was not without success was sufficiently proved in the person of his son, who is a senator for life in the Canadian Parliament, now assembled in the Capitol at Ottawa.

As I listened to this story, which was told with the utmost simplicity, it was as if I had fallen upon one of our own veterans, who had himself, or whose father had, perilled his life for his country. It added to a certain confusion of mind that has been growing upon me ever since I crossed the line; for, hard as I may try, *I cannot feel that I am in a foreign country.* The people are too much like our own "folks"—they have the same Saxon features, and if I would speak with them, it is in the same dear old mother tongue. True, I meet, as in this case, with many a canny Scot, and am sometimes answered in an Irish brogue, though not so often as on the other side of the border; but these little idiosyncrasies of look and of speech only give a pleasing variety to what would otherwise be the monotony of common life. After all, we are but one people, and these natural affinities will draw us together without a political union. Indeed, any suggestion of the latter, it seems to me, is rather to be discouraged in the interest of a real and genuine harmony. Last year I was in Paris, and had the pleasure of an hour with Lord Dufferin, whose splendid career as Governor-General of India has not abated in the least his interest in the country of which he was Governor-General before. In the course of conversation he asked me if there was a party in the United States that was trying to bring about the annexation of Canada? To this I answered without hesitation, "No," adding that, if in the course of time there should be a natural gravitation towards each other, which should end in a union that was not forced, but spontaneous, no doubt our country would be very proud of this accession to its greatness, but that it was not a question in American politics, and that such a thing as an annexation party did not exist; that on the contrary we were perfectly content to let things remain as they are, living in the best relations with those on our northern frontier. He thought it better that there should be two countries and two governments than one, in which many of our most thoughtful observers will agree with him. Our country is certainly big enough to satisfy any reasonable ambition, and it were but madness (and nations, like individuals, are subject to fits of insanity) to go on swallowing up "all creation." But we should not be so ready to agree in his opinion that the government of Canada is better than ours, and still less in one reason that he gave for it, that it is "*more democratic.*" But if we reflect a moment, we shall see that there is some foundation even for this; for while the Governor-General is appointed by the Queen, yet both in Canada and in England itself, public opinion acts more directly upon the government than in the United States. If the House of Commons were to pass a vote against the ministry to-night, Lord Rosebery would resign to-morrow; but Congress might pass any number of votes against the policy of the present administration, and yet Mr. Cleveland would remain undisturbed in his seat, and keep his Cabinet with him, till the end of the four years for which he was elected.

But without discussing the relative merits of the two forms of government of Canada and the United States, the main thing is that the two countries should live in perfect harmony. To this it is not at all necessary that there should be a political connection. We may like each other all the better that our relations are unconstrained. Even brothers sometimes feel a little more at ease with each other, when they keep up separate establishments. I was happy to assure Lord Dufferin, to whom Canada owes so much, that on our side of the line, so far from looking upon the territory on the other side of the St. Lawrence as a Naboth's vineyard, there was among us the most generous appreciation of a country that in popular regard is second only to our own.

This expresses the general, if not the universal, feeling in the United States towards Canada. Certainly if there be any people on the face of the earth with whom we should live, not only at peace, but in relations of good will and mutual kindness, it is those at the North, who are our neighbors, as well as our kinsmen; whom the Ruler of nations has joined together by nearness of habitation as well as by ties of blood, since the boundary between us is one that unites as well as divides. Looking at the map of North America, we see how our very territory is interlocked by a chain of lakes which stretch out their mighty arms east and west, north and south, till the two great confederations have literally "locked arms" with each other—not like gladiators in deadly combat, but like kindred in a brotherly embrace.

These inland waters bring us much nearer together than would any approaches by land, because of the commerce that is always passing to and fro over them. The thousands of sails that skim the waves are so many white-winged messengers of peace, flying to and fro like doves to their windows. With such tokens of good will in the very earth and air and on the sea, who that loves his country, or that loves mankind, will not pray that the relations between Canada and the United States may become closer and closer; that, as we love nations that are far away, still more do we love those at our own doors who are bound to us by the closest ties of kindred, of race, of language, and of religion?

CHAPTER III

IN RUPERT'S LAND—THE HUDSON BAY COMPANY

Some years ago I was talking with the head of the great house of Harper and Brothers about countries that we had seen or wished to see, when suddenly, as if a new thought had struck him, he said, "One region that I want to see is that lying on the Red River of the North!" I should not have been more surprised if he had expressed a desire to "interview" the King of the Cannibal Islands. What and where was the Red River of the North? I had a vague impression of some outlying part of North America, away up towards the North Pole, where in days gone by there had been a petty rebellion got up by a half-breed (in whom the savage instinct of the Indian had been made more quick and fiery by an infusion of French blood), which Lord Wolseley, when in command in Canada, had made a forced march, from Fort William on Lake Superior through the wilderness, to suppress. But that was not a thing to be remembered any more than a plague of grasshoppers. And now here I am standing on the bridge that crosses that unknown river, and wondering "where I am at." It is not much of a river, and, indeed, seems conscious of its inferiority, as it shuns observation, turning away from the more populous south and hiding its littleness in northern wilds and woods, till it is almost buried in ice and snow.

And yet here is a town—or rather let me say a city,

for it has thirty thousand inhabitants—which has a history dating back to a period long before our Western cities and States were heard of. Its appearance is, indeed, rather of the new order of things, after the pattern of our young cities of the West, of which the leading feature is one long wide street, with here and there a pretentious building intermingled with cheap wooden structures. The two that are most conspicuous are the Town Hall and the Northern Pacific Hotel, that great trans-continental line having stretched out one of its long arms to touch the rich wheat-fields of Manitoba. But the new jostles us almost painfully when we step into an electric car and ride through the one long street to the bridge that spans the chief arm of this mighty Red River of the North. As I walked slowly across it, and looked down upon the stream (that has not even the recommendation of a rapid current to compensate for lack of volume), it was with the feeling of disappointment that I once had in Nova Scotia in riding through the Acadia which Longfellow has described in his Evangeline, when I was amazed that out of such slender materials the poet could construct such a paradise of beauty.

And yet the poet may be wiser than the dull, prosaic traveller. He sees things which the latter does not see, and, gathering up the threads of history, throws over scenes and characters the warm light of his imagination, and makes times past to live again.

And so Winnipeg, dull and commonplace as it looks, has a history that invests it with an interest that belongs to few portions of the western continent, as it was the chief post of the Hudson Bay Company, that mysterious power that for nearly two centuries held dominion over a large part of North America. Here is a romance, yet to be told in song or story. To begin at the beginning one would need to go back two hundred years and more. In the year 1670—only fifty years after the Pilgrims landed on Plymouth Rock—Charles the Second, *not* " of blessed memory," bestowed upon Prince Rupert, the famous cavalry officer who fought against Cromwell in the Civil Wars, the title to a large country in North America; how large or how valuable he probably did not know nor care. In those days even the geographers of Europe had but little knowledge of the unexplored portions of the habitable globe, and a king gave away a distant territory more readily than he would have parted with one of the crown jewels. Near the beginning of the century an English mariner, by the name of Hudson, had made voyages to the coast of North America, in one of which he discovered a noble river flowing to the sea, to which he gave his name; and, the year after, a bay farther to the north and farther inland, that was connected only by a strait with the Atlantic. The island at the mouth of the river was preoccupied by the Dutch, so that an English king could not give that away, but the bay was as undefined as the moon, and Charles tossed it to his gallant soldier as lightly as he would have put a ring on the finger of one of the lady favorites of the court. The wording of the patent is peculiar. It was to Rupert, from whom it was called "Rupert's Land," as he was to be its lord and potentate, and fourteen of his associates, who are fitly designated as "the Governor and company of adventurers trading into Hudson Bay;" and conferred a title to "the sole trade" in all the country round, or, as it was designated, in "all the lands watered by streams flowing into the Bay." Thus a hundred years before Wolfe fought with Montcalm on the Heights of

Abraham, while France still held the Province of Quebec and the navigation of the St. Lawrence, the English power extended far into the interior, the frozen north, which it reached by Hudson Bay—a long and roundabout way, since it is open only two months in the year.

This was a prodigious gift, as it conveyed a territory large enough for a kingdom, with all the rights of sovereignty; for, although the concession was nominally for purposes of trade and commerce, yet, in a wild region where there was no established authority, the new Company had to assume, as a matter of necessity, the right to make laws and punish crimes, and so, with the Hudson Bay Company, as with the East India Company, the trading corporation grew into a government that by degrees became possessed of despotic power.

How absolute this power might be, not only over the natives, but over its own subordinates, is illustrated in the strange history of a man still living, whose name is honored in every part of the Dominion. More than half a century ago a young Scotchman came from his native land to take a place in the Hudson Bay Company, which (we cannot doubt from what we know of his character) he served with scrupulous fidelity. Yet one day an Indian runner came to him with an order to leave his post *in one hour* (he was not even permitted to wait to pack his clothing, which he was informed would be sent after him) and betake himself to Labrador! This was like an exile to Siberia; yet no explanation was given. The reason was a profound mystery. Yet for him who received it there was but one course—that of instant obedience;

> Not his to ask the reason why,
> His but to do or die—

and he obeyed. Without a word of remonstrance he left the place where he had begun to feel at home, and betook himself to a distant and inhospitable shore where he was kept for twenty-three years (!) when, on the death of the Governor, he was recalled, and as he had borne himself with the utmost fidelity in all this trying time, he rose quickly in the service of the Company, and finally became its Governor, an office which he still holds, sitting in the seat of the very man who sent him into exile!* His elevation did not upset him now any more than his humiliation before. He came back, not soured and embittered against the world which had treated him so harshly, but with all the sweetness of his nature kept fresh and pure. In his new position he grew in the esteem of his countrymen, so that there is to-day no name more honored in all the Dominion than that of Sir Donald Smith.

Here is history and mystery, with all the elements of a poem or a tragedy. Where could be found a more fascinating story than this of a commercial enterprise that began to be in a very modest and quiet way, as a company of traders or "adventurers," engaged in collecting furs, an occupation which led them to employ hunters

---

* In mitigation of this apparent harshness, an old settler said to me: "What seems like cruelty may not have been so intended. But the Hudson Bay Company was a sort of military organization, which had to be governed by military discipline, and ordered its subordinates to distant stations and perilous services, not as a punishment for offences, but as posts of danger which could only be held by those who had the true spirit of a soldier. The very fact that it was a post of loneliness and privation made it a post of honor, in which the young and the brave might find a path to glory and to power, as it proved to be in this very case, when, after twenty-three years of faithful service, he came back to take the highest place of honor and of trust at the head of the Company."

and trappers, whose very business was in the silence of the northern wilds, and yet whose masters were all the time creeping forward through those wilds, with the soft, catlike step of the beasts that they hunted, stealing towards power, till at last they held undisputed dominion from the Lakes to the Arctic Circle? With such a background of nature, and such a mingling of races, savage and civilized, it needs but a poet or a historian to set the figures—red and white, priest and warrior, in full array —and make the "sheeted dead" stalk across the stage of history.

But history and mystery fade away as we leave Winnipeg behind, and have before us a very substantial reality in the mighty plain that reaches from the water-shed of the Great Lakes to the foot of the mountains that border the Pacific Coast. The formation of this vast plateau is a problem for the geologist. It is not undulating like our western prairies, but level as a sea floor, which perhaps it once was. In some prehistoric period it may have been the bed of an ocean, which in the fullness of time was drained off through the lakes, leaving the soft and slimy ooze to be warmed by the sun till it was converted into a garden of fertility. But, whatever the explanation, the fact is here of a plain of boundless extent, which is one of the granaries of the world, the wheat fields of Manitoba vying with those of Minnesota, the value of which is multiplied tenfold as the production of the earth is increased by inventions of man that are mightier than himself. The great operations of agriculture are wrought by a hand that is longer and stronger than that of man—a hand that never tires—the iron hand of machinery. In these inventions the late Mr. McCormick has been a benefactor to his race. They seem to cover every form of labor, and to leave to man only the intelligence to direct. When the sower has scattered the seed and planted it, and the showers of heaven have watered it, then come the great harvesters, the mower and the reaper and the binder, to reap and gather into barns the harvests that will feed untold millions. With such implements of industry to multiply the forces of man, it is hard to put a limit to the productions of these boundless plains.

This is a sign of hope on the horizon of the future. So long as the country is but thinly peopled, it is of less importance than to the future generations that will yet fill this vast domain. To them it will be of infinite moment, for first and last the living world must be fed and kept in being by dear old mother earth. Egypt was made populous by the amazing fertility of the valley of the Nile, as the Tigris and the Euphrates fed the swarming multitudes of Nineveh and Babylon. Reasoning from such examples, we should say that this mid-continent may yet support a population like that of China.

But for the present China is not here. The land is indeed swept and garnished for the coming millions, but it will be far in the next century before they will take possession. Settlements are sprinkled here and there along the road, but (with the exception of Brandon and Portage la Prairie, the centres of the wheat-fields) they are so few and small that one is oppressed with a feeling of loneliness, to which it is a relief to see now and then a farm-house in the distance, and hear "the watch-dog's honest bark." It is pleasant, too, to see the herds cropping the rich grass, though we cannot speak of " the cattle on a thousand hills," for the hills are not here, though the cattle are.

But the landscape, taken altogether, is tame and monotonous in the extreme. To most of those who pass rapidly over it the absence of towns and villages takes away the only objects on which their eyes could rest with pleasure. What can they make out of a country that is as flat as Holland, without the picturesqueness of the quaint old towns, or the windmills and canals? To judge from the recumbent postures in which my fellow-travellers are stretched in these "sleepers"—a word that has an equal fitness to the long railway carriages and their occupants—their one desire is to get over the ground as quickly as possible. For this long-distance travel, the Canadian cars are better than ours in "the States," in that the middle seats of the drawing-rooms are so turned about in the daytime as to be converted into sofas, on which wearied travellers can stretch themselves, instead of being obliged to sit bolt upright all day long. By this convenient *siesta* they are refreshed for the long and delicious twilight that comes in the cool of the day. The proof of the excellence of this arrangement is that, after five days' riding, night and day, I did not feel the fatigue more than from much shorter journeys at home.

But apart from the fatigue, the mere monotony does not weary me. I am so "contrary" in my tastes, that what they count the dullest portion of this long journey is to me the most restful; what is tiresome to them has to me a peculiar fascination, so that I whisper to myself (what they would be shocked to hear), "Thank the Lord, there is nothing to see in a thousand miles!" Nature loves contrasts. A week ago I was in New York, which I left sick and tired of crowds and of the noise of city streets, and desiring nothing so much as silence and solitude. And here I find it. There is no fever in the blood, but perfect rest of eye and ear, of nerves and muscles and brain.

Nor does the time pass heavily, for I am never less alone than when alone. If I have no companions, my thoughts will keep me company. It is enough to sit and look out of the window, when the clouds flying over the sky seize my fancies and carry them away to other scenes and other experiences. If the sun is going down, sinking in the plain as in the sea, I remember an evening hour on the desert, when, mounted on my camel, I looked across the Red Sea to see the sunset flame over the mountains of Africa. Again, this vast plateau answers somewhat to the idea I have formed of the Steppes of Asia, and I imagine myself riding over the Siberian railway, that is yet to do for the greatest of continents what this Canadian Railway, with our own transcontinental lines, has already done for North America. So the hours do not pass wearily, but only in a happy dream, to which the gentle voice of one beside me is no interruption. Is there anything in the sunset of life so sweet as these golden hours when even old men dream dreams and see visions?

But if these be day dreams, what are those of the night, when the firmament itself seems to shut down close on the horizon; when heaven comes down to earth; and in this pure atmosphere, not clouded by the smoke of cities, the stars shine as on the desert! Then one's meditations take on a more sober hue; we think of the distant and the dead, and in such loving and inspiring memories get strength for what remains to us of that pilgrimage of life, of which all our journeyings are but a part and a preparation.

It was the afternoon of the second day from Winnipeg that we came to a place of some importance, that bears the singular name of Medicine Hat, derived, we believe, from some tradition of an old medicine-man among the Indians. It had a pleasanter association for us in our meeting here with Mr. Niblock, the assistant superintendent of this division of the road, to whom President Van Horne had given us a letter, and who joined us at Banff, and gave up three days to be our companion and escort.

We were now getting near the end of the mid-continent, and even the most listless travellers were beginning to open their eyes and prick up their ears in anticipation of what they were to see and hear on the morrow. Once in the night we were awakened at Calgary, where, looking out, we saw dimly a station built of stone, a sign that we were getting into the region of increased habitation and civilization. Calgary, the very name of which is English, is the centre of what is largely an English colony, made up of representatives of excellent families at home. Some of these true English gentlemen (for such they are by birth and by education) we met, with members of their families; and we could but admire the brave spirit of the high-bred sons and daughters of England, who had left the beautiful homes of the dear old motherland and crossed the sea to make a home for themselves and their children in the New World. And now the train was astir with the announcement that we were to have a change of scene; and soon all were in a state of excitement as, in the gray of the early morning, we entered the passes of the mountains.

CHAPTER IV

BANFF AND THE ROCKY MOUNTAIN PARK

THE mountains welcomed us with the sound of waters. It is the beautiful way of nature to beguile us into the heart of her mysteries. Somewhere up in the clouds a spring bursts forth and straightway seeks to return to mother earth, and, as it presses outward and downward, makes a path for its soft, silver feet, that widens and deepens, till, in the lapse of ages, there is an open passage on the mountain side. In this nature serves the purpose of man; for, as the stream winds hither and thither to reach the lower levels by gentle courses, it unwittingly indicates the path of the engineer, who, if he would scale these mighty barriers, has but to go up where the stream comes down. Almost all railways that cross mountain ranges find a pass through following water courses, by which they not only gain the easiest ascent, but follow the curving lines, which are the lines of beauty. This is the peculiar charm of railways in the Alps—a charm that we felt at daylight as we were running along the bank of the beautiful Bow River, which leaps from the mountains every morning and greets the traveller with as much warmth as if it had never seen a traveller before, and beckons him to the sweet odor of the pines and the first gleam of sunrise on the rocks and hills. As we enter these mountains, we find that the Canadian Pacific Railway Company (with a due consideration, not only of the comfort of passengers, but of the pleasure of tourists) has placed at the end of the train an observation car open at both sides, from which we have an unbroken outlook in every direction. Now we shoot through a narrow pass, where high cliffs frown on us from either side, as if we were invaders who had no business here; and though

"Stone walls do not a prison make,"

it would be depressing to live where one would be in deep shadow twice a day, at the rising and the setting of the sun. On our left is a triplet of peaks that bear the pretty name of the Three Sisters, to whom, having respect to their sex, we uncover our heads, and offer our morning salutation, but are pained to observe that, though they belong to the same family, and must have seen each other's faces every morning for some thousands of years, yet they stand apart as cold and distant as ever! It would seem as if there had been a family quarrel, and they couldn't get over it. This is a sin against nature. If they had been three brothers we could understand it, for they might have been estranged by their rival ambitions. But for sisters it is too bad. And yet here they are, with no signs of relenting, and we fear that, with the proverbial obstinacy of the sex, they will keep it up

"To the last syllable of recorded time."

We see no help for it, and must leave them, as we leave other "good haters" who "never will give in," to their mournful isolation and eternal solitude. With such merry fancies, as well as straining eyes, we are whirled swiftly along, till, while it is still the early morning, we draw up at Banff, and descend from the train in which we have come all the way from Montreal, a distance of two thousand three hundred and forty-six miles!

"Banff!" And what is Banff? And where is it? And why should we at this point break the course of our transcontinental pilgrimage? "I rise to explain."

Canada has had the wisdom of following in some things the example of the United States. We have not been always wise. Sometimes we have been very unwise; and in nothing more so than in the reckless and lavish way in which we have thrown away the public lands. To this national folly there have been two exceptions; in setting apart the Yosemite Valley and the Yellowstone Park as public reservations, not to be invaded by land sharks or speculators, or even by settlers, but to be kept sacredly for the people of the country, to be to them and their children "a possession forever." So the government of the Dominion, finding on the line of the Canadian Pacific Railway a region in which mountains are piled together in masses, sundered by deep gorges, decided not to throw it open, like other public lands, to the first settlers who should rush in and cover the mountain sides with their mining camps, but to keep it for those who could appreciate the grandeur of its Alpine scenery, or derive healing from its mineral springs. For their benefit this Rocky Mountain Park has been reserved as an inheritance for all generations.

Of this reservation Banff is the centre and the soul. But where did it get its name? There is such a place in Scotland, not far from Aberdeen, which is described as "a fine town," and sends a member to Parliament. What more natural than that this old Scotch name should be transported across the sea? Perhaps it is better to let it remain so, for a more searching inquiry might disclose a less sacred origin, one informant telling me that in the old Gaelic " banff " signified **"sheol,"** which would indicate that this region might have been so named by some disappointed settler **because** of its savage wildness, that **unfitted** it for **the** habitation of man, and should be set apart **as a sort** of Gehenna, **to be** occupied only by the outcast and **the** unclean!

But I hear a **whisper in my ear:** "Not quite **so bad** as that! Don't you remember that** he added, that, while such was the original meaning of the word, yet in common **use it** signified only a wild **and** broken country? **And surely** any one who should come up suddenly on these **rugged** mountains might well think **that he had reached** the jumping-off place."

That is **a good** suggestion, and relieves us of an unpleasant association. A word less strong may be admitted, especially when we see how quickly the picture is reversed; for, if any rough old Highlander had **it** in his heart to bestow an ill name upon this mountain fastness, he would be surprised indeed if **he could** open his eyes to-day, for here he **would see a hostelry such as Edinburgh** could not show when **I first saw** it. Come **in, my** good man **with** the tartan! **Just step** inside the door! See that huge fireplace, and **the** logs piled high, and the flame that roars up the chimney! Did you ever see the "like o' that" in any baronial hall in Scotland? Surely you never saw anything brighter or better. **And if you have** adhered to the custom of the Highlanders to **go with** bare legs, you may not be averse to standing **before** that fire till the warmth penetrates your very **bones.** Whenever I enter that hall, I cannot resist the temptation to turn my back to the blaze, for, though it

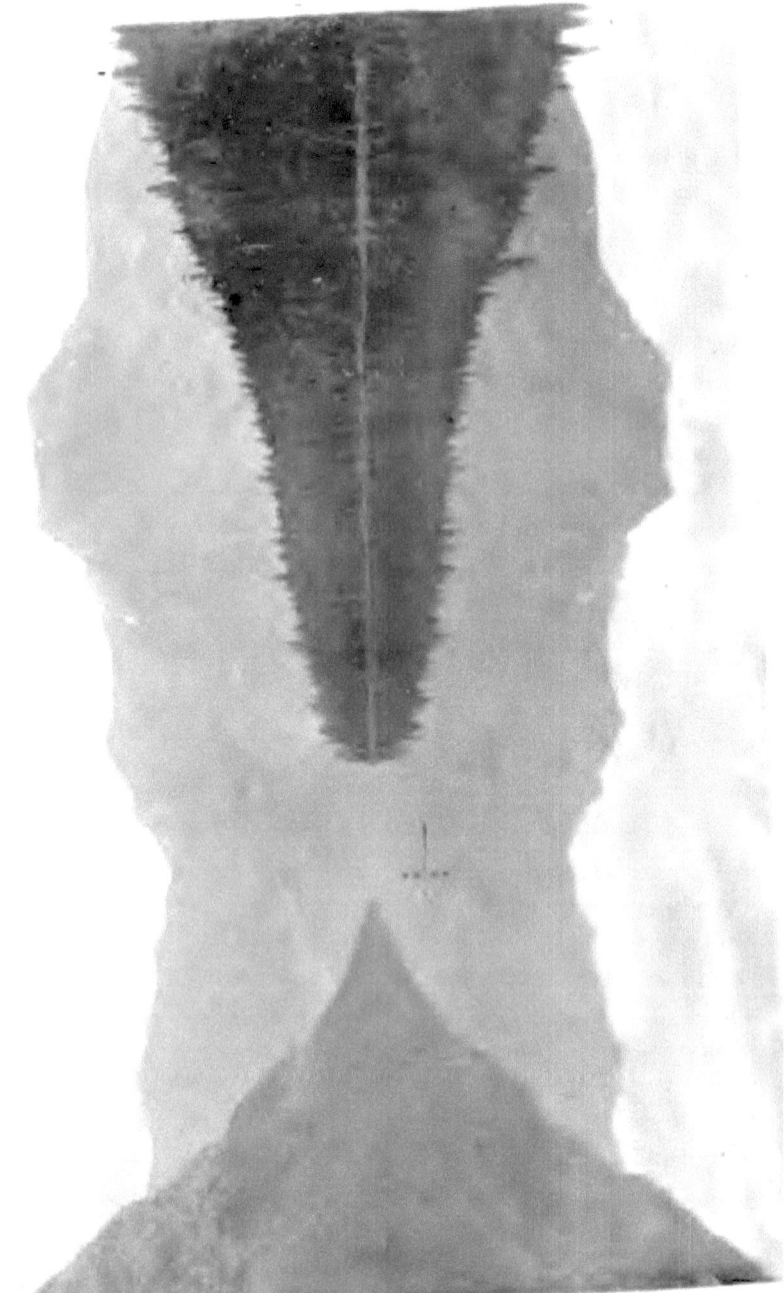

is almost midsummer, yet at this high altitude, forty-five hundred feet above the level of the sea, the air is still "frosty but kindly."

Thus this mountain retreat is made, not merely for show, but for comfort. The Banff Springs Hotel is a resting-place for the traveller, such as he finds only in the best summer resorts of Scotland or of Switzerland, with the additional attraction of its famous warm springs. It was a luxury indeed to throw aside our travel-stained garments, and plunge into the soft, delicious sulphur baths, and emerge in due time, clothed and in our right minds.

When we had thus been warmed and clothed and fed, we came out to survey the landscape and see where we stood. The position of the hotel has been chosen for its outlook. It is perched on a shelf of rock, which projects over the valley below, while it is at the same time in the very centre and focus of an amphitheatre of mountains. From my window I look down into a deep gorge, where the beautiful river "foams and flows," till it plunges into the depths below; and as the mist rises into the air, if the rays of the sun dart through it, a rainbow arches the abyss.

But it should be understood that this Rocky Mountain Park, though patterned after the Yellowstone, is by no means such a wonderland; it has no geysers, nor cañon, while in extent it is but little more than one fourteenth as large, the exact dimensions being twenty-six by ten miles in the one, to sixty-five by fifty-five in the other, making two hundred and sixty square miles as against three thousand five hundred and seventy-five! But there is no need to go into comparisons, for though this park be smaller than our own, it is large enough for a marvellous combination of grandeur and beauty, as it is filled with mountains, excepting only the gorge, through which the waters have forced their way in the lapse of ages, widening to a valley, round which the guardian summits keep watch in a mighty circumvallation of perhaps fifty miles. There is an advantage in having so much beauty and grandeur in a small space. One cannot do justice to the Yellowstone in less than a week, as it requires five days' driving from point to point, sleeping each night under a different roof; whereas here everything is within such easy distance, that all can be taken in excursions from which the parties return to the one central place of rest, and have a house-warming every evening, when all gather round the one hearthstone, and, before the blazing fire, talk over the adventures of the day.

With such attractions close at hand, I am not surprised that many come to this Park, not for a hasty glance, but to settle down for a whole vacation, as Eastern families spend their summers in the White Mountains. Only the last season a friend of mine, who lives in New York, made the long journey with his wife, and spent two months here, living out of doors, sailing on the lake, or driving or riding on horseback, and found in this mountain land such variety of scene that he was never weary of it. Ask him to-day for the place on all the continent where one can find the most of pleasure and of health, and he will point you to this Rocky Mountain Park as the very garden of paradise.

But one who comes only for a brief visit must make the most of his time, and should the last new-comer look upon me as an old resident, because I came two days before him, and ask, "Where shall I go?" I answer, "Go anywhere; you cannot go amiss. The chariot is at the door, and the mountain roads are excellent; jump in and let the horses fly!" You will not go a mile before you will ask the driver to draw rein that you may take breath, and let your eyes sweep round the horizon.

If I were to name one excursion as better than another (though perhaps it is only because it was the longest and the last), it would be to the Devil's Lake, in which I find nothing infernal but the name. It is a nine-miles drive from the hotel, where, at the foot of the mountains, we come upon a sheet of water that reminds me of the Dead Sea, in that it is so deep-set in the everlasting hills. The Dead Sea, as all travellers know, is the lowest body of water in the world, being thirteen hundred feet below the level of the Mediterranean. The depression of this lake is, of course, nothing to that, but it is still so deep down in the earth that its calm surface is like a sunken mirror in reflecting the awful forms of the heights that look down upon it.

But to see it in all its beauty, it is not enough to walk along its shore; one must sail over it; and as it is fifteen miles long, it was fortunate for us that there was a tiny steamboat, with a man and a boy to steer it and to feed its little engine, which puffed and wheezed as if it had the asthma. But no matter; it was big enough for three of us, and, seated under its little awning, we floated over the waters, that were so clear that we could see to a great depth. It was a sea of glass, in which, as in a mirror, the firmament above was reproduced in a firmament below, with clouds floating across the sky, and great mountains hanging downwards in that netherworld.

One bold headland is christened Gibraltar, and its majestic front is not unlike that of the Lion Couchant.

But those who dwell in this Alpine region need not to borrow greatness from a name, for in these mountain masses that sweep all round the horizon there are cliffs and crags enough to make a hundred Gibraltars.

But that which fills me with awe is the loneliness. It is the perfect solitude of nature, in which man seems like an intruder; so that when we looked up and saw on a tree-top a grand old eagle, he stirred not from his nest, but looked down with perfect indifference upon the little creatures that skimmed the waters below, while he with one broad stretch of his wings could sweep the heavens above us. Thus the birds of the air teach us humility. We feel the attraction that drew poets, like Southey and Wordsworth, to choose their homes amid lakes and mountains. If one could but live in such a presence as this, it seems as if he would be more than content to spend a good portion of his existence far from the madding crowd, the noise of which is kept away by the barrier of mountains, until the peace of the scene should pass into his soul. As we rode back when the shadows were falling, the mountains that we had passed but a few hours before seemed to have grown since morning and to reach up higher towards heaven. I had to lean back in the carriage to let the eye take in the summits, which seemed to soar and soar—oh, so high, and so far —above this lower world of sorrow and of pain! On their "bald, awful heads" were deep drifts of snow, that caught the rays of the setting sun; and now and then came on the ear the dull, but deep and thunderous, sound of the avalanche. That evening we sat a long time on the terrace in front of the hotel, looking round upon a scene that it was worth travelling more than two thousand miles to see; watching the twilight that was fading on the mountain tops; and even in the night watches, when I awoke, it was with a happy consciousness of being in some enchanted region, where, even while men slept, nature still chanted her low, deep anthem of praise, as all night long the cataract filled the mountains with its muffled roar.

CHAPTER V

HOW WE KEPT THE FOURTH OF JULY

IT was the morning of Independence Day that we left Banff, which, of course, made our hearts beat more quickly, though it did not give us a feeling of homesickness, and so abate our pleasure in the beautiful country where we were. It only added to the exhilaration of the mountain scenery and the mountain air as we drove down into the valley and over the iron bridge that spans the Bow River, while behind us the sound of the waterfall grew fainter and fainter. The sun had just risen, and touched the tops of the mountains on which we looked round for the last time. But we were not quite so lonely as we had been, for Mr. Niblock was an invaluable companion and guide. As he was always finding something new for us, he now suggested, as the train rolled into the station, that we should change our point of view from the observation car in the rear to the engineer's cab in the front, and thus look forward instead of backward. The change had its advantages, but I confess that I felt a little nervous at being thus promoted to a position which, if it was the best point of observation, was also the point of greatest danger. In travelling by rail I prefer to take a back seat, somewhere in the middle of the train. But my young companion was so eager for the new sensation that I had to yield, and we walked forward and were introduced to the engineer, Corey, more familiarly known on the road as "Charley," who had dismounted from his high seat and was standing on the platform. Niblock had whispered to us that he was a great favorite of Sir William Van Horne, who is a keen observer of men, and took to him, not only as a first-rate engineer, but as having an intelligence that made him a very pleasant companion to talk with, when the President came over the road. As he stood before us, we saw a stout-built man, with a slouch hat, and a sort of tarpaulin rig to protect him from the mixture of dust and oil to which he was exposed. Of course his face was somewhat grimed with smoke, but that did not hide the two sharp eyes that looked straight into the face of a stranger to "size him up." If I did not produce much impression on him, my companion did, for no sooner did he see her bright face, so eager and expectant, than he sprang into his cab, and reaching out his strong hand, lifted her up as gallantly as a sailor would swing a fair lady up the side of a ship, while I went round and climbed up on the other side. The quarters were not roomy, as the middle space was filled with the boiler and the furnace, into which the stoker was shovelling the coal, so that the air, which was already like the breath of an oven, grew hotter and hotter. We made ourselves as small as possible, so as not to be in the way. This may be ascribed to politeness, but I have observed that most persons are ready to give a wide berth to a steam-engine or a boiler that may explode and blow them into smithereens!

As there was some delay in detaching a special car at the other end of the train, Corey took the time to introduce us to his engine, for every engineer has his own, and this, though it had no name except its number (466), was to him like a living creature, which he had known ever since it came into the world, " when it was a baby," and which he had taken in hand as he would a bright and lively, but somewhat awkward, boy, who only needed training, and had trained it till it was his joy and pride. He spoke of it with a softness and tenderness of voice that showed that he loved it as the Arab loves the steed that sleeps under his tent; and to hear him talk you would think that the engine knew its master, as the horse knows his rider, and responded to his lightest touch as it would not to the touch of a stranger.

His one rule in training was that if you wanted "her" (for I think he always gave his favorite the feminine sex) to do her best—if you would get the most out of her, "you must treat her well;" for an engine that has done service for a good many years gets to be like an old man, a little rusty and stiff in the joints; and you must look after her, and see if she has not a lame foot, or is weak in the knees. In that case she should be rubbed down as you would rub a blooded horse that you wished to keep in prime condition, and be well oiled in every spot where she is a little sore. By this constant inspection and loving care for the dear old creature, she could be "limbered up" and kept in repair, so as to do still more years of service in going up and down these mountains.

When he had done all this, and polished her off so that she was as fresh as a daisy, he stood off and looked at her with a smile of satisfaction that seemed to say, " Old girl, no matter how many daughters there may be, thou excellest them all!"

While talking with such animation Corey put his head out of the window every minute to see to the side-tracking of the special car, all the while keeping his hand on the throttle, so that he could with the slightest pressure of his finger move forward or backward. When this little side matter was adjusted he turned to his steed that had been champing at the bit, and gave a little stronger pressure, and the long train began to move. At first very gently, for his quick eye saw that I was not quite so much at home in his cab as I might be in the pulpit; and out of condescension to my infirmity he moved off so slowly that all my nervousness was lulled to rest, and I straightened up with a jaunty assurance that showed how indifferent I was to this sailing through the air, which was as gentle and quiet as if we were in a boat gliding through the water. While I was thus patting myself on the back as a man whose nerves could not be shaken, Corey turned round to another face that was right behind him, and seeing it glowing with eagerness, he just whispered to the "old girl," and opened the throttle and "let her go!"

Goodness! how the old lady danced! It was a Virginia reel! In less time than it takes to tell it, she sprang from her slow pace of ten miles an hour to fifteen, twenty, twenty-five, thirty, thirty-five, forty, and forty-five! This, he told me afterwards, he did "just to please the young lady!" Ah yes, this was very well for the young lady; but how about the old gentleman? I thought my hour had come! For a few minutes I felt as if the Old Nick himself had got me (as the darkeys would say, "shuah"); yes, had got me by the nape of the neck, and was rushing me forward to some place where I didn't want to go! But after keeping this lightning gait for ten or a dozen miles, he slowed up a little, by which time I had become accustomed to the speed, so that the nervousness was all gone, and the sense of danger was changed to one of pleasurable excitement; and at the wind-up, when we had made the run of thirty-six miles to Laggan, I was not only at ease in the engineer's cab, but was ready, like Oliver Twist, to ask for more! As we stepped to the platform, I thanked our new friend (for as such I shall always think of him) for a novel experience that was one of the most pleasant in all our journey to the Pacific.

When we waved our hand to the engineer, as he bore away to the west, the scene changed from the flying car to the stillness of the forest; for Laggan, though once a busy spot when the road was in construction, is now only a gateway to something better than itself. The only inhabitants are a few Indians (who furnish ponies to tourists), with their squaws and pappooses. Knowing that they are a shiftless race, idle and lazy, and often thievish, I took for granted that they must be very poor neighbors. But the station-master told me that they were far better than the average white men whom I should find on the border, for that, poor as they were, not a man would touch a thing that was not his. Whence this honesty that hardly belongs to any race so low in condition? It is all explained by the fact that years ago a Scotch missionary, John McDougal by name, came here, and (instead of swinging round the circle once in three months, like a circuit-rider, to blow a blast under the trees, and then mount his horse and disappear in the woods) he came to live among them, to share their privations, to be with them in summer's heat and winter's cold, and thus by his patient teaching, and, above all, by his own example, he won them to habits of honest industry, and to pure, Christian lives.

While listening to this, the Indians were saddling the

ponies, and soon we were all mounted and following one another in Indian file up the mountain. As we moved off in silence, we were in some excitement in hope of an adventure. The woods are said to be full of bears, and if one should but cross our path, what a story to tell our friends at home! Only I fear, if Bruin had thrust his black nose out from under the trees, he might have set our hearts beating with a sensation that was not unmixed enjoyment!

We had not gone far before the ponies gave a start, and drew back as if they snuffed danger in the air. Alas, it was only a porcupine! But as it was climbing a tree, it looked as large as a bear's cub, and with its quills that in an instant might stand out like a hundred spears, it was not a creature to be handled lightly. The sudden apparition gave us all a start, but Mabel's one sorrow was at the loss of the opportunity to show her skill as a shot. In our peaceful Berkshire home she had sometimes toyed with a pistol, or even with a small gun, and now deplored her fate that she had not " her rifle " to bring down this mighty game, for want of which she had to leave it to the Indian who followed her, who, without waiting for a rifle, or even a bow and arrow, picked up a stone from the road, and despatched it at a blow. Much as I regretted her disappointment, I thought it would not be proof of an unerring aim to shoot a poor beast that was so near that she could touch it with the muzzle of her gun, nor that even a bristling porcupine, hung up in the ancestral halls at home, would quite establish her fame as a second Diana, a huntress of the forest!

But no hunter's fancy could divert us, but for a moment, from the exquisite beauty of that ride in the woods, through "the murmuring pines and the hemlocks" and along the border of a stream that rushed over its rocky bed. Thus, winding slowly upward for three miles, we had risen a thousand feet, and came out on a terrace, on which stood a Swiss chalet, overlooking a scene that was thoroughly Swiss in its combination of lake and mountain, though the lake takes the name of an English princess, who is an enthusiastic lover of the wild and beautiful in nature, and who had opportunity, during the years that her husband, the Marquis of Lorne, was Governor-General of Canada, to study the scenery of America; and surely in all that she saw from Montreal to the Pacific, she could have found nothing more worthy to bear her name than the sheet of water that now opens before us, which has long been a favorite subject for artists. "Some years since," said Mr. Niblock, "I came here with Mr. Albert Bierstadt, who, as he came to this spot, threw up his hands in ecstasy, exclaiming with an enthusiasm that only an artist could feel: 'Never have I seen anything to approach this before,' and, lest the vision should escape him, he seized his pencil and began a sketch before the picture should vanish out of his sight." While the Indians unsaddled the ponies and let them rest under the trees, we sat on the veranda, taking in the features of the scene, which fortunately can be grouped in one view, since Lake Louise is not, like the Devil's Lake at the Park, long and winding, so that while viewing one end the other is out of sight, but is so shut in that the eye can take in the whole from a single point of observation. The picture is framed for us, as if by the hand of an artist, somewhat in the shape of a triangle, of which the chalet is the apex, while the two sides that broaden from it are two mountains, the one on the right somewhat sloping and covered with a dense forest, and the other a bold rock over two thousand feet high, rising perpendicularly, like the dome of El Capitan in the Yosemite Valley; while the third end of the triangle, which faces us at the farther end of the lake, is one enormous glacier that literally covers the mountain with its slopes and pinnacles of ice and snow.

As we shall return to this central spot and take another view from the lake itself, as we sail over it, we leave it for two or three hours to make a still higher ascent. Once more the ponies are saddled, and, passing round the lake to the right, we climb up another mountain steeper than the last, till we look down into the clear waters of what is fitly called Mirror Lake, as it almost startles us by the vividness with which it reflects the rocks and hills. So complete is the illusion that we had to withdraw our eyes and look round us, to be sure that we had not been turned upside down, and left with our heads hanging downward to the earth!

At this height—indeed, with its very base above the level of Mirror Lake—is a mass of rock called, from its shape, the Bee Hive, around which we crept as carefully as if we were every moment expecting a stinging salutation, and when we reached a point where even our surefooted ponies, that can almost cling, like chamois, to the side of a rock, could go no further, we had to dismount and climb, not only with our feet, but our hands, seizing every projecting bush, or limb of a tree, by which we could pull ourselves upward, till at last we reached the level of a third lake that is literally in the clouds. This is Lake Agnes, which is three thousand feet above the level, not of the sea, but of Laggan, from which we set out in the morning.

And now, having got up, it is almost as difficult to get

down. For part of the way we trust only to our own feet, picking our way very cautiously, with hands outstretched to seize any means of support, and when we take to our ponies, and they put out their fore-legs, we expect every moment to be pitched over their heads. However, as we submit to the necessities of the occasion, and are willing, for once, to "go slow," the Lord preserves us, and by special mercy we find ourselves again at the chalet, in front of which a couple of Indians, whom we left behind, are telling stories of their bear hunts, in which, though they speak in their native tongue, their features and tones of voice show that they feel all the excitement of the chase.

And now, having had so much of poetry and also of fatigue, an hour of rest is not unwelcome, especially with the substantial lunch, for the Swiss chalet is not merely a picturesque object in the landscape, but an excellent house of refreshment for the weary traveller, that will give him new life to enjoy the sail on the lake. The landlord of the chalet is a skilful oarsman, and the boat glides softly over the waters. Now it turns to the right, and skims along in the shadow of the forest. If any visitor is not content with scenery, and must have his gun, let him "take to the woods," and he may stir up a bear before the day is ended. As we have no such ambition, we prefer to keep on to the farther end of the lake, where we are to have our first near view of a glacier. From the chalet it presents only the appearance of a mountain covered with snow. But as we draw nearer, its character defines itself more clearly, the beach being strewn with stones and fragments of rock swept down in avalanches, from which the snow has melted, leaving this wreck and ruin along the shore. Behind this rises a mighty wall of ice in strata like those of a rock-ribbed mountain, piled one above another, till there must be literally hundreds of thousands of tons, pressing forward and downward. It is well that the lake is here to receive it, for if men had ever built their habitations on the shore, as Italian peasants have built on the sides of Vesuvius, they would share the same fate.

But this great wall of ice, that hangs midway on the mountain's side, does not reach to its top. Behind it and above it a vast snow field rises against the sky—the Great White Throne of the Eternal Majesty.

When we are ushered into one of these great scenes of nature, the first impression of beauty, or even of sublimity, soon gives way to something deeper, which touches our poor human lives. In this close contact of nature and man, the greatness of the one is placed in sharp contrast with the littleness of the other. As we turn away from this dazzling brightness, we sink into an insignificance that becomes almost annihilation as we sweep round the lake to the wall of rock on the other side. As our little skiff glides into the shadow, the boatman drops his oar, and we float in silence, not saying a word, but looking up speechless to the tremendous cliff that hangs over us as if to crush us. And indeed it would crush all hope within me, if I had no religious faith, by its awful weight and its infinite duration. Other mountains than Sinai speak to us—what has this to tell? It tells us that we are of yesterday and know nothing, while it may date its beginning from the foundation of the world. What then is human existence in the presence of this Ancient of Days, that has looked down on a thousand generations, and will look down upon a thousand more?

And yet we find another Presence here; for if we come out to-night when the stars are shining, we shall see them reflected in the waters, so that whether we look upward or downward, we shall find a firmament above and a firmament below, and be looking into the very face of God!

Then tell me if you will that life is but a bubble on the ocean:

> "A moment white, then gone forever."

But even if a bubble bursts, the drop of water which for a moment it held in air is not lost, but sinks into its native element, to roll in the waves till there is no more sea. And is not our little life a part of the universal life, of the life of God, to whose all-embracing bosom it returns and there liveth and abideth forever? Such was the comforting reflection that I brought out of these great scenes of nature, and took to my poor heart, as I rode silently and thoughtfully down the mountain side.

CHAPTER VI

RIDING ON THE COW-CATCHER

WHEN a man of uncertain age starts off on a trip across the continent, it would be rather dreary for him to go alone; and he is fortunate if he has in his family one (of the proper age and sex) whose young eyes may brighten his lonely hours. Especially if he is a little dull himself, or is subject to drooping spirits, the sight of another in whom life is fresh and strong may react upon the heaviest heart. Sometimes it reawakens life in one who is a trifle "past age." This process of rejuvenation cometh not from within, but from without. It is not enough for a man to look into a glass and see himself, but other eyes must look into his eyes, and another heart set his heart beating faster with a new pulsation of life and of happiness.

But there is nothing in life that has not its reverse side; even in joy there is a shadow of pain; and youth, from its very excess of life, sometimes crowds upon the lingering steps of age. The sweetest disposition may have behind it a strong personality; and a fairy young creature may have a will of her own. This may explain a discovery which I made on this journey (of course, no uncle ever discovered it before)—that my delightful travelling companion had some tastes that were, to say the least, peculiar. Hardly had we gone beyond the bounds of civilization, before she confided to her uncle that her one ambition in life was to ride on a cow-catcher!! to which he answered sharply, "Nonsense! Ridiculous! Absurd!" telling her that it would be highly improper and even dangerous, and what was worse, that it was unwomanly—it might do for a cow-boy, but not for a well-bred young woman—and tried to divert her mind by asking her about the new books which she had read, and telling her to look out of the window at the grand mountain scenery! She listened silently, casting down her eyes like a nun, and yet for an instant he thought there was a faint twinkle in them, that indicated that she would bide her time.

The time did not come till we had crossed the plains, and entered the mountains. But when the Fourth of July had fully come, Americans, even though on British territory, feel that they must do something for the honor of their country—perform some exploit which, if not revolutionary, is at least unexpected. We had begun the day by riding in the cab with the engineer; we were to end it by being projected out of the cab upon the cow-catcher!

When we came down from Lake Louise, and dismounted from our Indian ponies at Laggan, which we had left in the morning, we found ourselves once more on the line of the railroad, but no train stood there to receive us. There is but one through train a day— that which had brought us in the morning—and had we been "common folks," we should have been stranded here to wait till the morrow. But the Superintendent was all-powerful, and anticipating the difficulty, in the absence of anything better, had ordered, for the stress of the occasion, a hand-car such as is used by the workmen on the road. There it stood, with four lusty fellows to serve in place of an engine. Of course, it was not imposing to look upon. It was not as gorgeous as a gilded howdah, in which I have sometimes sat on the back of an elephant, which moved forward with a majestic tread that warned everybody to get out of the way.

But handsome is that handsome does, and this plain truck sufficed for the occasion. Here we took our seats like

"Three black crows all in a row,"

Mr. Niblock and I nearest the wheels that we might have the lady member of our party between us for her protection, though she laughed at the idea of danger, or rather, to put it more strictly according to the fact, thought "a spice of danger would give zest to the ride," and almost screamed with delight when the sturdy wheelmen put their strong arms to the task and bowled us over the road.

But I did not feel so sure of my safety. The old line says,

"They that be low need fear no fall."

But I am not so sure of that, for our danger was in the very fact that we were low, since our feet were lower still, and as they swung in the air, I was in constant fear that they would strike some piece of rock that had fallen on the track, and send us all flying from our seats, with the car rolling over our heads; and it was with entire satisfaction that, after a run of eight miles, we came to the end of that part of our journey.

Stepping from the track to the roadside, we found that in that eight miles we had completed the last stage in our ascent of the Rocky Mountains, and now stood on the very point of the Continental Divide. Leaping up the grassy bank, I found rippling over it a swift-running stream, not too large for me to bestride like a Colossus, in which Herculean act I outdid the Colossus of Rhodes, as I stood with one foot in the Northwest Territory, and the other in British Columbia, and literally straddled the waters of a continent, since at my very feet the stream divides into two, one of which flows north and east, to wander here and there down the mountains and through the valleys and over the plains, till it rests in Hudson Bay; while the other turns to the west, to sleep at last in the calm Pacific.

But what goes up must come down. Having climbed to the crest of the mountains, to the dividing ridge, we must make an equal descent on the other side, and to get down safely we must go slowly and pick our way with judicious care. It would hardly do to trust our lives to a hand-car, which might soon acquire a velocity that could not be held back by any hand-brake; and the Superintendent, who was equal to all emergencies, had ordered up an engine to take us on board. Now came the opportunity for which my young companion had been waiting to enforce her request to take the advanced position of which she was so ambitious. It looked as if there was a conspiracy against me, for I now remembered that the week before, in Montreal, when Sir William was dictating to his secretary the points of interest for us to see, he let drop the remark, "Perhaps Miss Dwight would like to ride on the cow-catcher going down the Kicking Horse Cañon!" Ah! there it was, and whether he had passed the word along the line to Mr. Niblock, I did not know; but here was the fact right before us that an engine was standing on the track, with steam up, but *no passenger car!* How were we to

KICKING HORSE CAÑON.

ride? There were but two ways—in the cab with the engineer, as in the morning, or on the cow-catcher in front! This was the alternative for which my little maiden had waited. Her time had come! How could I resist any longer when her plea was enforced by the necessity of the case? So at last the young lady carried her point over the old gentleman. Mr. Niblock wished to oblige us both, yet in his heart I think he leaned to the other side, and I don't blame him. And so the "old man" came down, as he was in duty bound (for what are old men for if it is not to come down on such occasions as this?), and the men went to work with a will. Everything had been prepared beforehand. In front of the boiler were some projecting braces, that seemed to have been put there to support a piece of timber. Upon these was now lifted a heavy railroad tie, and when it had been made fast and strong, will you believe it, "His Reverence" was the first to exalt himself to this position of dignity, taking his seat in front of the boiler, with his arm round his young protégée, while the Superintendent and the conductor seated themselves so as to keep the balance even. Thus projected to the fore end, I was no longer merely a king on the back of an elephant, but a *mahout* sitting on his very head, thus to be swung down the valley, unless perchance (as elephants, like men, sometimes go crazy) he should get impatient of his burden, and, with one toss of his head, throw us over into the gorge below.

The excitement of the situation was increased by another circumstance—that we were to feel our way down the steepest grade in the Rocky Mountains, two hundred and thirty-eight feet to the mile! Of course, the engine was not needed to draw us forward, but only to hold us back, for its mere weight on such an incline would give it a momentum that would increase every moment. And, as if this were not enough, the engineer took the opportunity to "hitch on" a long train of freight cars, which would increase the momentum to something frightful if anything should give way. Sometimes a train breaks loose and rushes down a mountain with fearful speed. That such a thing was not impossible here was shown by the provision of numerous sidings, with a man at the switch, so that, if the train should get unmanageable, a quick turn would whirl the head of the monster to one side, and off on a level track, where he could have time to think about it, before he renewed the perilous attempt. If all these precautions were to fail, and the train should rush madly down the mountain, of course we who were on the bow of the ship would be the first to go in the general smash, and would not be left to tell the tale!

Was it not then a piece of foolhardiness to expose ourselves to such danger? No! Because in fact the danger has been reduced to a minimum by the wonderful mechanism provided to control such a tremendous force—something to overcome the power of gravitation and hold this enormous weight, as it were, in the air. And here I take the opportunity, while crossing the Continental Divide, to pay my tribute to a man whom I am proud to call my friend, George Westinghouse, who by his air-brake has put a curb-bit in the mouth of the wildest steam-horse that ever dashed down a mountain or raced across a continent. But for him we should have to creep where now we fly. We should have to crawl at a snail's pace across the plains, and be let down from any height with extreme caution to secure our safety. With such liability to runaways, one could never feel safe in a railway train. To the great Wellington, the conqueror of Waterloo, the danger seemed greater than on a battle-field, so that for years after railways were introduced into England the old Field Marshal would not risk his life upon them. Nor was the Queen permitted to expose her royal person to a danger that seemed all the greater in that it was unknown. But our countryman has laid his hand on the power that threatened destruction, and its terror is gone. By a device which seems very simple now that he has discovered it and applied it, he has grappled and chained the steam-engine, and made it absolutely obedient to the will of man. With his air-brake he can hold half a mile of cars, going down the steepest pass in the world, or stop any "lightning train" when rushing forward with frightful velocity. For ten long miles we were descending this cañon, but not for an instant did this wild courser of the mountains break from the hand of its master, who, by a simple pressure on the brake, could hold the mad creature as in a vice. With such airy security did we descend, that, had we been favored by the presence of the Jubilee Singers, I should have asked them to sing one of their wild melodies:

"Swing low, sweet chariot,
We are coming along home!"

And home it was when we were all set down at the foot of the mountain, in a quiet valley, without a single jar, or a moment of fear or anxiety.

Thus we celebrated the Fourth of July by a grand performance in four acts: riding in the cab with the engineer; riding on Indian ponies up a mountain to what are fitly called the lakes in the clouds, and down again;

riding on a hand-car; and riding on a cow-catcher down the steepest grade in the Rocky Mountains!

But could we not have been let down from that height with just as much ease and more comfort if we had been sitting inside a Pullman car? What was gained by putting ourselves on the outside? We sometimes take a world of pains to do what is not worth the trouble, just for the satisfaction of having done it. Was not this all that we had to show for this foolish exploit? The reader shall judge.

We were at the top of the Continental Divide, and the gates of the Rocky Mountains were opening before us. The Cañon of the Kicking Horse River is one of the wildest and grandest in all that mighty range. If the river had not taken its name from some incident that happened to one of the early explorers, it would still have been not inappropriate, since it is always flecked with foam, and rushes on in such wild fury that it seems to be kicking up its heels into the air. It is at once a Destroyer and a Creator. In the lapse of ages it has fought its way through the mountains, and in its deep gorge cleared a passage for the steps of man. On either side the scarred and broken cliffs are the monuments of its tremendous power. Between these cliffs, down this gorge, and on the bank of this rushing, roaring river, we were now to descend.

Of course, the first necessity was to have the view unobstructed. There is all the difference in the world between craning our necks out of a window, or even standing on a platform, turning this side and that to catch glimpses of all this grandeur, and being in the very focus of the whole, where we can take it all in with one sweep of the eye. Perched on our " coign of vantage," there is nothing between us and the mountains, which crowd into our very path, so that we can almost touch them with our hands. In going down such a pass the sensation is very different from that in going up, when we are all the time rising into the light of the open sky, while here we are sinking, sinking, till we can almost say with Jonah, "I went down to the bottom of the mountains; the earth with her bars was about me forever." As we descend lower and lower, the mountains rise higher and higher, and their snowy peaks shine brighter and brighter in the face of the sun. Is not this the glory of the Lord upon the mountains?

And now what do I think of riding on a cow-catcher? I have to confess that what I looked upon as a childish freak has proved a revelation; that the child was wiser than the man; and that to youthful enthusiasm I owe one of the most thrilling experiences of my life.

At the end of the cañon the picture is made complete, and, as it were, "framed in" by two giant mountains. Mount Stephen is not the highest peak I have seen in the world, but it is one of the grandest in its majestic form, as its wall of rock rises like a fortress, throwing out its buttresses on every side, till it is a very Gibraltar in the clouds, with its banners floating in the sky; while in the centre of it, and rising still higher above it, is a huge mass, the shape of which suggests to every beholder a cathedral of the Middle Ages; and he must be dull and insensible who does not feel stirring within him some sentiment akin to worship as he looks up to its pinnacles and towers.

But when the day was over, and we were at the pretty English inn that is nestled in the valley, with a green lawn in front, and a fountain playing, I looked across the river to the mountain on the other side with a feeling that was more tender, as it bears a familiar name that was given to it many years since, when my brother Cyrus came through this pass in company with one of the projectors of the Canadian Pacific Railway, in honor of whom the mountain just described was christened Mount Stephen (and who, having since been raised to the peerage, has taken back the name as his title, and is now known as Lord Mount Stephen), who himself proposed, in respect for one who had done so much to unite England and America, that the sister mountain should be called Mount Field. It is according to the fitness of things that these two Alpine heights should stand facing each other, as perpetual memorials of the friendship of those whose names they bear, and of the work which they did, each in his way, to promote the peaceful intercourse of mankind.

All this came to me as I sat in the twilight, looking up to that snow-clad peak, on which the sunset lingered, and found comfort to my sad heart in thinking that, though my brother had passed out of my sight, in this new empire which is rising on the Pacific Coast, one of the most commanding summits in all its great ranges would preserve to future generations his beloved name.

MOUNT FIELD.

CHAPTER VII

THE GLACIER OF THE SELKIRKS

AT THE FOOT OF MOUNT STEPHEN.—Dear, dainty dell! Dropped from the clouds into the heart of the wilderness! Yet not quite like the gentle dew from heaven, or the rain upon the mown grass, but only when the skies are wooed and won by the loving toil of man. Nature had provided only a river, which, finding its level at the foot of the pass, overflowed its banks in the springtime, when the snows melt upon the mountains, and, cutting out a little space from the nearest slope, made a few acres of level ground. But it was not till the sturdy woodman came and laid his axe at the root of the trees, that sunshine was let into the gloom of the forest. Then long trains brought loads of rich soil to spread over the barren surface, and so in due time a bit of Old England was indeed "dropped from the clouds" into the heart of the American wilderness.

But the picture would not be complete without the English inn. The English—in whom we include their descendants on this side the Atlantic—are the only people in the world who understand the full meaning of the word comfort. The French excel in show, in architecture and in decoration, but for the interior, give me the English home and the English inn, with its open fires and "creature comforts," to restore the vitality of the wearied traveller. It was good to find such a haven of rest at the close of the Fourth of July, our celebration of which, if glorious, was somewhat fatiguing. Personally I did not mind it, for I count myself an old soldier in the grand army of travellers. But the case is different with a young recruit, whose very ardor may spur her to exertions beyond her strength, and for once I felt real anxiety. But a warm bath and good soft bed are great restorers, to which I trusted, and not in vain.

Thus relieved from my fears, I returned to the veranda, and, looking up at the mountains, questioned the very intelligent landlady about the life in this corner of the world.

"It must be very lonely here in the winter?"

"Yes; though we see a little of the world every day."

The trains bound east and west both stop for half an hour, the one for breakfast and the other for supper, so that she saw new faces and heard new voices, but what was it? A stream that swept by like the river before her door and vanished into vacancy! She said:

"They come and go, and we never see them again."

The solitude, it seemed to me, must be increased by the position in a valley shut in by high mountains, above which the sun rises "behind time" in the morning, and sets "before time" in the evening; thus shortening the day at both ends, so that the night is longer, and the day shorter, than on the mountain top or in the open plain.

"But have you no neighbors?"

"Only those employed on the railway; wood choppers who cut down trees for railroad ties; or workmen who keep the track in repair."

"And do you never have unexpected guests?"

"Yes; sometimes we have a flood of people, for whom we can hardly find places to sleep, or food to eat. Only two months ago the washouts to the west swept away bridges and embankments, so that the track was broken in many places; for weeks they had to carry passengers in boats up and down the Fraser River, till the track could be repaired. As it was broken quite near us, the course of travel was stopped at this point, and the reports sent abroad were very alarming."

"I remember having read in the New York papers that a Raymond party was lost!"

"Yes," she answered, "and at that very time that very party was here at 'Field,' safe under this roof, and subject to no greater hardship than detention on their journey. But as days passed by the number of storm-bound travellers increased till there were a hundred and sixty! Of these, however, sixty were Chinamen, who could be bestowed in the adjacent cabins and fed with whatever could be found for them, while the hundred had to be squeezed together as closely as possible to find places for them to lie down, and supplies for the table. But everything was done that could be done for their comfort during the time of this enforced delay, while the whole expense was borne by the Canadian Pacific Railway Company."

This incident shows that the inns which the Company has built through the mountains are not intended merely to be picturesque objects in the landscape, nor even hostelries for travellers, but life-saving stations also, as much as those erected on a stormy and rock-bound coast for sailors who are in danger of perishing by shipwreck. They are houses of refuge as truly as the hospices on the top of the Alps—on the Simplon and the Great St.

Bernard—for the rescue of those who might otherwise be buried and lost in the snow.

As work must be dull at times, both in summer and winter, it occurred to me that the woodmen might take to hunting, and I asked:

"Is there game to be found in the woods?"

"Oh, yes," was the answer, "and you need not go far to find it. There are bears all over these mountains, and other wild animals. Only a few days since I was on the other side of the river with a friend, and through the trees we saw a pair of sharp eyes fixed on us. At first I could not make out what the creature was, but looking more closely till my eyes could get accustomed to the darkness, I saw that it was a lynx" (a sort of wildcat, that is said to grow to a larger size in Canada than anywhere else in North America).* "He did not trouble us, and, of course, we had no desire for his company."

As the winter is, of course, the most difficult season of the year to work the railroad, I was anxious to know if the passes were ever blocked by storms; if the snow line hung low on the mountains; and if avalanches, or "snowslides" as they call them, ever descended into the valley. The track, I find, is here, as on our own Pacific roads, protected at exposed points by snow-sheds, which sometimes extend for great distances, whose steep roofs catch the drifts as they fall, over which they slide into the gorge below.

And as to the avalanche, the terror of Alpine villages, surely that never comes here! The snow-banks lie so

---

* The Canada lynx, the *loup-cervier* of the French Canadians, is said to be the largest specimen of **lynx in North America**. It lives in the deepest woods, and rarely approaches human habitations.—*Appleton's Cyclopedia.*

peacefully on the mountain's breast, dripping away in drops that trickle down the mountain side, and glide away in rivers to the sea; surely nothing in nature ever looked more innocent. What is so light, so feathery, as particles of snow? Is there anything that falls so gently, and rests so lightly on the bosom of mother earth? It is the one thing in nature that we choose, as we speak of the down of the swan, as the emblem of lightness and beauty and grace. We should as soon think of finding terror in a butterfly's wing, or a robin's song, as in the beautiful, beautiful snow. And yet, what do I hear to-night? That the bank of snow that gathers on yonder mountain top, if once loosened from its base and set in motion, will come thundering down the mountain side as a destroyer of everything in its path, breaking off the thick trees as it would sweep over a field of grain. And as for the thunder of its voice, a year or two since an avalanche descended from Mount Field, the concussion of which (increased, perhaps, by being thrown back from Mount Stephen) was so tremendous, that it broke every window in the hotel!

The next morning the young traveller, for whom I had been so anxious, appeared after her night's rest as fresh and bright as ever; and as the train from the east came in, turning out its load of passengers for breakfast, the solitary place was filled with life and gayety. In an hour we were on our way, and so full were we of the exhilaration of this mountain air, and so determined to see everything, that we took our places again in the engineer's cab, where I now felt so much at home that I even did the honors of this new reception room, and gave my seat to a couple of friends from New York, while I stepped outside and stood by the boiler, holding on by the rod that serves for the firemen or brakemen as they may need to pass up and down. I cannot say that I should always choose this outside passage, but for once there was the same excitement in it which a landsman finds in climbing to the masthead, from which he can look down upon those on deck, but from which he is happy to descend as soon as possible.

And now what were we to see? The day could not be so rich in experience as yesterday, for that was the culmination of grandeur and beauty. And yet the last word of Mr. Niblock as he left us in the evening was: "*Tomorrow you will begin to see mountains!*" What did he mean? To me it seemed then—and seems now—that, familiar as he is with all the peaks from the plains to the Pacific, the mere succession of one after another, the fact that " Alps on Alps arise," gave him, as it would give any traveller, the impression that he was himself rising higher and higher. Whatever the explanation, the fact is that we make our triumphal march across the continent over three great ranges, which, fifty years ago, when little was known of their geography, were grouped together under the general name of the Rocky Mountains, a term that is now restricted to the first range, which we have just crossed; while beyond us are the "Selkirks" and the "Cascades," the latter including the great mountains on the coast. It is the second of these —the Selkirks—with which we are now to make our acquaintance. We have not to go far to find them, for here they are in all their rugged grandeur! Hardly have we turned our eyes from the Cathedral of Mount Stephen before we see on the western horizon the Van Horne Range, a mighty battlement of mountains, standing up against the sky, as if to bar our passage to the

Western Sea. By what feats of engineering this cloud-capped fortress was stormed and taken, it would be a thrilling story to tell. Mountains are not to be "stormed" as were the Heights of Abraham. They can only be taken by the slow process of siege, working round on this flank and on that; and if still kept at bay by precipices too high to be scaled, and too broad to be flanked, attacking them in front, boring into the rock-ribbed hills and making a tunnel perhaps miles in length, till the loaded engine that has been standing on the heights above, chafing with impatience, is at last let loose, and, advancing through fire and smoke, as if making a charge in battle, issues, like some wild monster escaped from prison in the bowels of the earth, and rushes madly down the side of the mountain. Such was the achievement here, one of many proofs of the boundless energy of one man, who did more than any other to carry through the daring and magnificent enterprise of the Canadian Pacific Railway, in honor of whom this lofty range fitly bears his name.

With such an introduction to the Selkirks, I began to think that Mr. Niblock had not overstated the matter when he said, "Tomorrow you will begin to see mountains," as we climbed steep ascents, one after another, and at times seemed for a few minutes to be suspended in air, while we crept slowly over a bridge that spanned some mountain gorge, from which we looked down into the abyss below.

So rapidly did these scenes succeed one another as almost to fatigue the eye, and we were not sorry to break our journey again for a day of rest at Glacier, which, like Field, is set in a deep valley in the heart of the mountains. In their general features the two places are alike. Both have their green lawns and sparkling fountains. But one feature Glacier has which Field has not—a stream pouring down the face of the mountain (which stands over against it), and lighting up the dark background of the forest. This reminded me instantly—as it must remind every one who is familiar with Swiss scenery—of the Staubbach in the valley of Lauterbrünnen. One difference there is, which varies the scene. The Staubbach descends in a single leap, with nothing to break its fall, and before it touches the earth is dissolved in spray; while here the silver current comes down in a series of cascades that keeps the stream unbroken to the end. In both waterfalls there is the charm of contrast with the surroundings, the ever-flowing stream taking on new life and beauty as it flashes over the eternal rocks, and its dashings mingle with the murmur of the dark funereal pines.

In this enchanted valley is the inn, which has one advantage over that in which we slept last night—that, as at certain seasons it is a resort for hunting parties, it has an annex, which doubles its capacity for guests. In this we found not only large private rooms, but a spacious parlor, of which, as by good fortune it was not occupied to-day, I took possession, spreading out my books and papers, and doing my reading and writing as if I were in my own library. In this delightful place of rest we spent twenty-four hours.

But, of course, the first duty of a traveller, in coming to a place far off in the wilderness, is to see the sight which has made it famous. The sight here is the great glacier of the Selkirks. As it must be approached on foot, which involves a good deal of fatigue, I excused my young lady from the attempt, and left her to her rest, while I accepted the offer of the landlord to be my guide, and taking our staffs in hand, we set out, as if we were two pilgrims on our way to the Delectable Mountains.

We had not gone far before we saw proof of the destructive power of an avalanche. On the other side of the valley, through which the glacier forces its way, is a mountain covered with forest, where it seemed as if all the snows of winter might fall, hardly breaking more than the twigs of the trees. But only a few years since, the drifts were piled so high that they broke loose and came down with the fury of a cyclone, cutting off trees two feet thick like saplings. Nor did the avalanche stop when it had reached the foot of the mountain, but swept across the valley, and some distance up the slope, on the other side, carrying destruction before it. This is a big story, and I shall not be offended if some of my readers shake their heads in doubt, for, in truth, I should hardly believe it myself if I had not seen with my own eyes the wreck it made.

From here the path leads across a stream, which, as it never ceases its flow, indicates the inexhaustible source which it finds in the glacier by which it is fed. Climbing slowly upward, we come at last to the foot of the glacier, whose first appearance is disappointing, as one sees no tall cliffs of ice shining in the sun, nothing but a vast snow-bank, strewn with all the débris of winds and storms. Coming up closely to it, I first mounted one of the great boulders that lie in front of it, and took a view from a respectful distance. Then, getting bold by familiarity, I came nearer, till I laid my hand upon it, as upon some fearful power that I hardly dared to touch, and in a foolish freak threw myself down and crawled under it, and even tried to woo the creature in whose power I was by putting my face against the glistening surface above me ; but it made no response—its kiss was cold as the lips of death. Then crawling out again, and returning to the rock, I looked the grim monster in the face, and asked, " What are you? How long have you been ploughing this mountain side, and how long will you continue your work of destruction?" As to its substance, anybody can see that it is an enormous mass of ice and snow. But how great is it, and how long has it been accumulating? That bank is probably hundreds of feet thick, and it may have been piling up for hundreds of years! As to its extent of surface, we see only what reaches to the top of the nearest ridge ; but if we were to climb to that spot, we should see that it stretches far away over other heights, and down into valleys, till one can hardly say where it ends. I believe the men of science reckon it to be fifteen miles long.

And this is not a dead mass, powerless and motionless, but is moving on day and night, with a power hardly less than any of the forces of nature, unless it be that of the ocean itself. And even the "cruel, crawling foam" of the sea is not more "cruel" and "crawling" than the " foam " of the ice and snow, beneath which are the ever open crevasses of the glacier, presenting so many slippery paths to destruction. Seeing what a part it plays in these mountains, we are more ready to accept the theory of an Ice Age, a Glacier Epoch, when masses of ice, large as islands in the sea, swept over continents, changing climates, and even the formation of the globe. Into all this I do not enter, but one lesson I find here (preachers are always looking for lessons): that in the material world law works inexorably, whether to create or to destroy. The forces of nature are but the outward manifestations of that power of the Almighty which is behind them all. If the sceptic will not listen to one speaking from the Bible, let him go out on this mountain side, and mounting some huge boulder that was thrown down ages ago by a force that is as mighty to-day as it was then, he may take it for a type of the weight and force of the moral law, of which all material laws are but types and emblems, and say in sad solemnity: "Whosoever shall fall on this stone shall be broken, but on whomsoever it shall fall it will grind him to powder."

CHAPTER VIII

TO VANCOUVER AND VICTORIA

GLACIER, where we spent such a restful day, is a place of meeting for the trains, which do not glide by each other in darkness, like "ships that pass in the night," but stop in broad day for dinner, so that travellers from the east and the west meet on the same platform and at the same table for a good half hour—more often an hour—time enough to exchange friendly messages, and speed each other on their way, after which they vanish :—

"Come like shadows, so depart."

But even in departing they linger a while in sight of each other, for the track here describes a loop that circles round three sides of a valley, so that the train from the west comes up on one side, and makes a graceful curve, as if it were with a bow and a curtsey to its sister, and swings round to the other side, where it continues its ascent to the top of the ridge; while the train going in the other direction reverses the movement, so that the two remain for some minutes in sight of each other, and friends who have already shaken hands and said good-by can wave a last farewell.

When this excitement was over, and we settled down into our seats, we began to realize that we were on the home-stretch in our long journey across the continent, and that one day more would land us by the waters of the Pacific.

We were now on the down grade, but we were not to come to the sea by one long continuous descent, but by a succession of ups and downs, whereby the perpetual variety is continued to the end. Among the wild scenes of the afternoon was the Albert Cañon, where a mountain stream has forced a passage that is hardly wide enough for itself, but in which the iron track has demanded room, and found it high up on the cliffs above. Here the train halts for a few minutes, that the passengers may walk out upon a platform and look down into a gorge three hundred feet deep!

We are now in the heart of British Columbia, and are coming down into the valley of the Columbia River, which we crossed at Revelstoke about the time of the going down of the sun. What a noble river it is, broad and deep, and flowing with a swift current! But have we not seen it before? Did we not cross it yesterday? But then it was running in another direction! We have read of "the inconstant sea," but here is an "inconstant" river. The Columbia rises in British Columbia, just over the border, and begins its course toward the north, and so continues for several hundred miles, till, as Sir William Van Horne playfully puts it, it "gets tired of it," and turns southward, and crossing the line, enters Oregon, and after a course of hundreds of miles, with ever accumulating volume, empties into the Pacific. So the Columbia belongs neither to the Republic nor the Dominion; neither can set up a claim to the exclusive possession of one of the great rivers of North America. It belongs to both. Let it wander where it will—north, south, east, or west—its windings hither and thither, carrying back and forth the commerce of the two countries, will be so many coils of a mighty chain to bind together two peoples whose race and language are the same, and whose true interests are one.

But hardly have we time to reflect about the Columbia River before we have crossed the valley and are up again into what is called the Gold Range, from the diggings that have been worked in it from an early day. But the attraction to a traveller is a succession of small lakes surrounded by the forest, in which we recognize the mighty trunks that we see in the Coast Range of California.

The next day was the last of the week and of our long journey. At North Bend we took our places in the observation car, for we had need of all our eyes, since the Canadian Pacific ends in a blaze of glory. The Fraser River is not so well known as the Columbia, but in scenery, if not its equal, it is, as the racing men would say, "a good second." Long before the white man came, it was known to the Indian, not as the happy hunting ground, but as the happy fishing ground, for its catches of salmon were the wonder of the coast. Indians still come to cast their nets into the stream. A touching proof of their former occupation is seen here and there in the grave of some old chief along the banks, where perhaps he had wished to sleep,

> "By the lone river,
> Where the reeds quiver,
> And the woods make moan,"

as if, "in his narrow cell forever laid," he might still hear the moaning of the winds and the murmur of the waters.

After the Indians came the miners, who, while prospecting and digging in California, had heard that there was gold to be found in British Columbia, in the sands of the rivers, and in the gulches of the mountains. Straightway they shouldered the pickaxe and started for the north, where they found access to the land of gold by way of the Fraser River. I suppose that there was an old Indian trail on the left bank, which the first white adventurers turned to account, making it wide enough for their loaded teams, beside which they plodded their weary way. But the railroad apparently disdained the old paths, and took to the right bank of the river, though it was forced, as it were, to "strike in the face" a succession of cliffs that line the river for more than twenty miles. Against these cliffs the track is bolstered up wherever there is a ledge for it to stand on, or a projecting point to which it can cling, and when all fails a way is cut through the living rock. We were all in a state of excitement, as we leaned out of the windows to look up at the crags above us, and then down at the waters rushing and swirling below. Talk of the Iron Gates of the Danube! They are not to be named beside the Iron Gates of the Fraser, which at one point seemed to close upon us, and to be barred and bolted, to forbid our passage. But our chariot of fire stopped not even to take breath, but rushed on, flaming and smoking, into the heart of the earth, and in a few minutes reappeared in triumph, careering down the valley, till the river gave it up, for as we crossed a bridge to the left bank, it turned to the right, and we saw it no more, while we kept on into a more open country, till at one o'clock we completed a journey of nearly three thousand miles!

Vancouver is itself not the least of the creations of

the great Company, by whose choice of it as the terminus of a transcontinental railway, it was at once foreordained to greatness. But the suddenness with which it has sprung into existence almost outdoes our own achievements. Ten years ago the place where it stands was covered by the primeval forest. But suddenly the wilderness was attacked by an army which had marched across the continent, and was flushed with victory. A hundred axes made the woods ring, and soon the mighty oaks and firs were laid low; and a town was hardly drawn on the map, before streets were laid out, and lined at first with woodmen's cabins, but soon after with comfortable homes, among which rose, in due time, many beautiful residences and fine public buildings. On the top of a hill overlooking the town is a hotel that in size and architecture would not be out of place in any of our Eastern cities. I need hardly say that it has been built by the same central power that built the hotel at Banff, and in pursuance of the same wise policy that has made it the first business of a company that provides for the public, to consider its convenience in every detail. Nothing could exceed the courtesy which we have met at every step of our journey from Montreal to Vancouver. Hardly had we reached the hotel, before the Superintendent, Mr. Abbott, called to see if he could do anything for our comfort. He took us about the town to all the points of view, on the best of which stands his own residence, with its foreground of lawn, and flowers in bloom everywhere; while the interior is filled with books and pictures, and all that makes the beauty of an English home.

Another feature of the town that will be of priceless value in the future is the reservation of a very large portion of its site for a park, which (thanks, perhaps, to the limited means of the first inhabitants) has not been spoiled by excess of floral ornamentation. The forest is left as nearly as possible in its native wildness, with avenues cut through the woods, and drives to points where one can get the best lookout upon the sea.

With such attractive surroundings, Vancouver is a beautiful termination of a transcontinental highway, which serves the double purpose of business intercourse and political union. Not that mere inter-communication can reconcile antagonisms created by war. A dozen railways crossing the Rhine could not make France and Germany friends. But where there is but one people, separated by great distances or high mountains, the breaking down of these barriers is the most direct means of fusing them together. *Our* transcontinental roads have brought the Pacific Coast nearer to us on the Atlantic; and what they have done for us, we should rejoice to have done for our neighbors on the north, who have not only shown a noble rivalship in enterprise, but have at the same time adopted a political union so like our own.

But Vancouver is not only the terminus of the highway upon the land, but the starting-point for a voyage upon the sea. Here are waters deep enough to float the largest ships in the world. Mr. Abbott took us on board the Empress of China, one of the great steamships that have been built for the commerce of the Pacific in connection with the overland railway. It was lying at the wharf close to where our train stopped, and we had but to walk across the platform from the one to the other, and need not (if we had so chosen) have even put our feet to the ground till we touched the soil of Asia!

And this new way across the continent is the nearest route from England to Eastern Asia. Eighteen years ago I crossed the Pacific as the last stage in a journey round the world. Then we came from Yokohama to San Francisco, the course to which seemed very direct. Yet what may appear on the map most direct may not be the shortest nor the quickest. To quote what I have written elsewhere : *

"We did not steer straight for San Francisco, although it is in nearly the same latitude as Yokohama, but turned north, following what navigators call a great circle, on the principle that, as they get high up on the globe, the degrees of longitude are shorter, and thus they can ' cut across ' at the high latitudes. 'It is nearer to go round the hill than to go over it.' We took a prodigious sweep, following the *Kuro-shiwo,* or Black Current, the Gulf Stream of the Pacific, which flows up the coast of Asia and down the coast of America."

In this "great circle sailing," we came past the latitude of Vancouver, which, though some degrees farther north than San Francisco, is really a day or two nearer to Yokohama, as proved by marine measurements and by repeated voyages. In 1876 we were seventeen days at sea, and thought it a quick passage. Now the English mails have been carried from Yokohama to London, crossing two oceans—the Pacific and the Atlantic—and the American continent, in twenty-one days! This is indeed bringing the ends of the earth together, when the farthest **west** looks across the tranquil Pacific to the farthest **east,** which this new means of communication has brought nearer than ever before, for which we say

---

* "From Egypt to Japan," page 421.

that its constructors "builded better than they knew." They set out to unite the British possessions in America, and have gone far towards uniting the world.

Here then, to use the words of the rousing old camp-meeting hymn, we "raise our Ebenezer"—we set up a milestone to mark the progress of the nations. Up in the mountains that we passed yesterday is a spot that every traveller can help to make historic by fixing the name and date, as a way of "driving a nail" where one was driven before on a memorable occasion: "At Craigellachie, twenty-eight miles from Revelstoke, the last spike was driven in the Canadian Pacific Railway, November 7, 1885!" That spike clinched the last rail in one of the greatest structures ever undertaken by man. Thereby hangs a story of constructive genius, united with indomitable courage and perseverance, which the world should not, and will not, "willingly let die!"

Vancouver is not an open port, looking out on the broad expanse of the Pacific Ocean. It is not so ambitious, but is content with the foreground of a peaceful inland sea, which lies along the shore of British Columbia, as Long Island Sound lies on our eastern coast. Beyond this western sound (to continue the comparison) rises an island, in position like Long Island, though farther out to sea, and of far more majestic proportions, as it is eight or ten times as large; and, instead of being low and flat—a mere sand-bank thrown up by the waves—it is dignified by a range of mountains two thousand feet high, with one peak nearly six thousand— far higher than Snowden, or any mountain in Great Britain. But this need not touch the pride of England, for they are all in British possessions. This outlying island was not left by accident in the midst of the seas, but was placed there by the Almighty hand for a purpose—to serve as a breakwater to the great ocean that lies beyond; so that if the typhoons of the China Sea were to send a tidal wave across the whole breadth of the Pacific, it would break harmlessly upon these rocky shores. It was fitting that such an island should bear the name of its discoverer, who, beginning his naval career under the great explorer, Captain Cook, after his death made other voyages to higher latitudes, where, just a hundred years ago, he discovered and gave his name to the most important island on the western coast of North America.

The impression of this distant view was greatly increased when we put out into the deep, and could at the same time look out on both sides, as we sailed down the Gulf of Georgia, with mountains to the right of us and mountains to the left of us, all aglow with the setting sun.

Crossing from Vancouver to Victoria is not like crossing the ferry to Brooklyn, for Victoria is nearly a hundred miles away, and it was after midnight that we saw in the distance the lights of the harbor, a half hour later that we were at the wharf, and two o'clock when we were at rest in our hotel.

But daylight, however early it may come, seldom finds me sleeping, and I was abroad at the peep of day to take a view of the capital of British Columbia. No change could be greater than that from Vancouver to Victoria. It was a transition, not from the old to the new, but from the new to the old; for, while Vancouver has not had ten years of existence, Victoria counts its full hundred.

The city was quiet and still, as became the day of rest. Among the public buildings are numerous churches, of which the Catholic is perhaps the largest, though the English is dignified by the name of a Cathedral; and as the morning drew on, it was pleasant to see the recognition of the holy day, in the people going to their different places of worship. Some of our party were gratified by a visit to the harbor of Esquimault, three miles distant, the place of rendezvous for the English fleet in the Northern Pacific, where they attended divine service on board the Royal Arthur, the Admiral's ship, at which the whole ship's company, officers and crew, attended with the utmost reverence, and joined in the prayers which were offered at the same time in the churches and cathedrals of dear old England.

Though Victoria is not a large city, it has a quiet, English dignity. Its streets are well laid out, and there are many fine private residences. As it is the capital of British Columbia, it has a colonial government, for which it is now erecting an imposing Parliament House, which, I take it for granted, will be the centre of all the public offices, and, perhaps, of the courts as well; so that it will be a sort of Temple of Justice.

But Victoria had an interest for me that was quite apart from all these; that was wholly personal, which I cannot introduce without giving a bit of history. I have already referred to the great service rendered by the Canadian Pacific Railway, in the work of confederation of all the British provinces of North America. Now that the thing is done, it seems the most natural thing in the world, and hence the most easy; whereas, it was for a long time earnestly and almost violently opposed. It was not a union into which all parts were drawn by an irresistible mutual attraction. On the contrary, the East and the West were as much divided as any two countries could be. They were not only hundreds but thousands of miles apart. The geographical centre was not the same as the centre of population. Hence, the indifference to union was greater as you came farther west, till at last the whole scheme was met with pronounced and determined opposition. It was all well enough (so the people reasoned) to have a grand Confederation stretching across the continent in order to gratify the pride of the East, which, having an immense majority of population, would take to itself all authority and power. But what good would it do to British Columbia? It would be merely the tail end of the kite, floating out on the waters of the Pacific. The people of this coast, though comparatively few in number, had the blood of England and of Scotland in their veins, and did not care to be swallowed up by the more populous East. If the older and richer provinces of Upper and Lower Canada were willing to undertake the enormous enterprise of opening a path through the illimitable forests, of bridging the rivers and scaling the mountains, well and good! Otherwise, British Columbia would stand alone, sitting like a queen upon the waters of the North Pacific!

Here was an opposition that required, not only political wisdom and sagacity, but great tact and a spirit of conciliation, to overcome. To meet the emergency the British government picked out from among its colonial governors one in the prime of manhood, who had already shown great ability as the Governor of Newfoundland, from which he was transferred to the other side of the continent. He found that the difficulties had not been exaggerated. It was not merely a desire for independence on the part of the people of British Columbia, but it seemed to them that their interests could best be promoted by keeping their separate government. On board the steamer from Vancouver I had been introduced to Mr. Justice Crease, who has lived in Victoria more than thirty years, and was at that very time the Attorney-General. He told me how the Governor had been injured by a fall from his horse, so that for some weeks he had to keep his room, where the Cabinet met beside his bed, and consulted how the obstacles might be overcome. One by one prejudices were removed, and the popular feeling conciliated. But still, after all, there remained one insuperable obstacle—the barrier which nature had interposed, in the distance which separated the West from the East, that was made the more formidable by the triple chain of mountains that had to be crossed. To this there could be but one relief, in an assurance that that obstacle should be removed by the construction of a transcontinental railway! That assurance he felt authorized by the Home Government, as well as by the Canadian government, to give. The condition was accepted, and upon this solemn assurance British Columbia surrendered her separate existence. She ceased to be. The Governor laid down his office, and returned to England. For this successful negotiation Sir Anthony Musgrave has sometimes been called the father of the Canadian Pacific Railway. But this he would have been the last to claim, for he was as modest as he was efficient when any work was to be done. It were more correct to say that the great enterprise had many "fathers," all of whom had a share in the great achievement, and should share in the honor, for surely there is enough for all.

But what have I do with it, that I should tell the

story? Only this, that when the Governor of British Columbia had accomplished the work which he had so much at heart, he had the further happiness that his beautiful home was brightened still more by the presence of a countrywoman of ours, who was the only daughter of one for whom the flags in the city of New York were but recently at half mast, Mr. David Dudley Field.

With such memories and associations I could not go away without seeing the home where lived one of my own kindred, and so, waiving all ceremony, I drove to the Government House, where the Lieutenant-Governor (British Columbia has no longer a Governor) welcomed me with true English heartiness and cordiality, and took me over the house. "This," he said, as we entered a large room full of sunshine, "was the favorite room of the Princess Louise, when she spent six weeks here." And then he took me out upon the grounds, which command a glorious view of the mountains and the sea. Yonder, Mount Baker stands alone, with its "diadem of snow," while on the other side of the Straits of Fuca is the grand Olympic Range. What a place of beauty to be filled with happy memories! As I left, the wife of the Lieutenant-Governor would have me take in memory of the place a bouquet of roses, saying, "Perhaps they are from a bush planted by the hand of Lady Musgrave!" These were pleasant memories, and yet they were mingled with sadness, for Sir Anthony Musgrave (after a long career of usefulness and honor, as Governor successively of Newfoundland, of British Columbia, of Natal in Africa, of South Australia, of the Island of Jamaica, and of Queensland) died a few years since at Brisbane, where he sleeps. But though men die their work lives, and it was to me a proud association with Victoria, that it once had been the home of one who had borne himself with such wisdom, such dignity, and such success, that his name here, as in so many other parts of the world, will long be held in grateful remembrance.

CHAPTER IX

THE GREAT AMERICAN ARCHIPELAGO

At last we are on the waters bound for Alaska! The first morning I was on deck early to see how we were to be provided for in our sea home. On the Pacific one does not expect the magnificence of Atlantic steamers, and yet, as I looked round, I was more than content with our new quarters. The Queen is a model steamer for inland waters, with accommodations that are the perfection of comfort. Some of us got more than comfort. My niece and myself each had a stateroom on the upper deck, but, as if this were not enough, she was promoted to a still larger room opening into the saloon, while I, who had left my better half far away in the East, was comforted in my loneliness by being installed in the bridal chamber! This was not comfort—it was luxury. Thus once more the lines had fallen to us in pleasant places.

But our luxury was not to the sacrifice of others' comfort, for everybody had ample room. This might not have been quite so easy if the ship had been overcrowded, as it is sometimes. For this very trip, it was said that over two hundred passages had been engaged, but scores were prevented from coming by the strikes which had just broken out, and that were especially violent on the western coast. A party from San Francisco, that succeeded in getting through, had a pitiful tale to tell of a blockade so close that not a train could move, and they had to take to the sea on the Walla Walla, in which they were so crowded that eighty-five had to sleep on the cabin floor! But "all's well that ends well;" and now that they were safe on board, they had the more elbow-room from the very fact that others had been kept away. But though the number was reduced by the strikes, we still mustered over a hundred passengers, a goodly ship's company. Of course, it was a miscellaneous gathering, but it proved a very pleasant one. For the most part, we were strangers to one another, and yet there were a few familiar faces: a party from New York that we had met at Banff, and a family from Brooklyn; and, nearer still, a lady who had a country place on our hill in Stockbridge, who, with her sister-in-law, was returning from a voyage to Japan and China, whose sudden appearance gave us at once the feeling of being with old neighbors and friends.

The deck of a steamer that is over three hundred feet long furnishes an ample promenade to take our "constitutionals." It served also as a sitting-room of ample dimensions, for it was covered with a double awning, which protected us alike from sun and rain; and here we spent the greater part of the day, stretched in our steamer chairs, book in hand, or in conversation with new acquaintances from this side of the continent, who were full of information as to its marvellous growth. But however engaged, talking or reading, I always kept an eye out upon the tranquil sea, and the mountains that looked down upon it. We were returning on our track in sailing up the Gulf of Georgia, but daylight gave us many a view that had been lost before in the darkness of the night. The mountains that we had seen dimly as mighty shadows, were now revealed in their rugged grandeur, as they stood up against the sky. The coast is indented by deep inlets or *fiords* like those on the coast of Norway, between which bold headlands jut into the "confined deep." The effect of this panorama of mountains and sea was heightened by the perfect weather and the cloudless sky. It was all a blissful waking dream, as we floated on silently and peacefully over the soft, slumbering seas.

So the day drew on, followed by the long twilight, and still we were not in Alaska! It was a disappointment to be told that it would be two days before we were out of British waters. This northwestern boundary of the United States had once been a subject of controversy with England, which roused such a feeling as to threaten war. Of course, the bare possibility of a call to arms was enough to fire the blood of Young America, and our youthful warriors aired their patriotic enthusiasm in the terrible alternative which they presented to England: "Fifty-four forty, or fight!" We had in command upon the frontier an officer who was in such a belligerent mood, that he was ready with half a dozen companies of soldiers to attack the British Empire! And indeed he came near getting us into trouble, for in those days there was no telegraph across the continent by which the government could communicate with those in command at distant points. How relieved we all were when the old hero, General Scott, sailed for Panama on his way to Oregon! As soon as he appeared on the scene, order was restored; and the two small bodies of troops on the border were not allowed to make war on their own account.

After all this bluster, it was rather humiliating to find

that, in the opinion of the best authorities, the territory in dispute did not belong to us, but to England! But it was to the honor of our country, that, when the proof was made clear, the point was yielded, not grudgingly and in anger, but gracefully; and forty-nine degrees of latitude—instead of fifty-four degrees and forty minutes—was accepted as the true northern boundary of the United States. This prompt acknowledgment was rewarded some years after (in 1872), when there rose another question, as to the channel in the waters dividing the two countries, which was referred to the Emperor of Germany, who decided in our favor, thus giving us the large island of San Juan.

But in spite of all this, I dare say that some of my countrymen, as they sail up the Gulf of Georgia, find their enthusiasm chilled by the cold reflection that all these woods and waters are not ours! In this feeling I do not share, nor would my enthusiasm be quickened in the slightest degree if the bird of freedom were soaring and screaming over every mountain top. It is nothing to say that we might have had this territory if we had had the courage to fight for it. Yes; that *might* have been, and it might *not!* Some may tell us that we got the worst of the bargain. No matter if we did. We got what was right, and we had rather be right than be victorious. But in fact the decision was for the advantage of both, whose supreme interest it was to be at peace.

At the time this territory was only a vast, unsettled region in the frozen north—a country without inhabitants. But if it had been the richest country in the world, we could not afford to take that which did not belong to us. The great interest of nations is justice;

and if there be a point on which they should stand upon their dignity, it is in a proud sensitiveness to national honor; which, if there be a doubt about a claim, would lean to the other side. If this be an excess of generosity, a little touch of kindness is not out of place between kindred. Might not Brother Jonathan say to his English brother, "What is that between thee and me? There is room for us both on this broad continent, and we may well be content to live side by side, at once the nearest neighbors and the best of friends."

Here ended the first lesson with the first day. The second was like unto it, for we were still in British waters, though not quite so much on an inland sea as when in the channel, which is smooth and unruffled because protected by Vancouver Island from the inrolling waves of the ocean. That breakwater, three hundred miles long, was lost when we passed out of the Gulf of Georgia and came into the more open Queen Charlotte Sound, where we were able, for a few hours, to look out on the broad Pacific.

The next day we crossed the parallel of fifty-four degrees forty minutes, which separates Alaska from British Columbia. At St. Mary's a single house with the American flag flying over it marks the dividing line, and we slowed up till the captain could go on shore and show that his papers were all right; and when we started again it was with the proud consciousness that we were in the waters of the Great Republic.

An American would not be quite himself if he did not experience some glow of feeling in coming into a region, however distant, that belongs to his country, and in part belongs to *him*. Every man in the United States is owner of Alaska, to the extent of one seventy millionth part of it. Wherefore it becomes him to look sharply at his new possession, with the interest which comes from a feeling of proprietorship.

He has the more reason to look, because Alaska is not like any other State or Territory. It has indeed a vast unexplored interior which has points of resemblance to other portions of our country. But what a traveller sees in an excursion to Alaska is simply what lies along the coast. And this is all described in one word — it is an Archipelago — a sea full of islands, in which it suggests a comparison with other archipelagoes in distant parts of the world. Of these I have seen the two most famous: the Greek Archipelago, lying at the eastern end of the Mediterranean, along the coast of Asia Minor; and the Malayan, at the southeastern corner of Asia, which includes Sumatra, Java, and Borneo, each large enough for a kingdom—a chain of islands that stretches away to New Guinea, and forms a sort of Giant's Causeway between Asia and Australia. But there could be no better illustration of the meagre interest created by mere size, than the little that most men know, or care to know, about the mighty Malayan Archipelago, as compared with the interest they feel in the little Greek islands, among which are such historic spots as Scio, where Homer lived and sung, and Patmos, where John saw heaven opened and wrote the Book of Revelation.

But Alaska has no history, except a geological history, which is of interest to men of science, as indicating the convulsions which have shaped this part of our continent long before man appeared upon the earth. The feature of this western coast is a chain of mountains, which, with its extensions north and south, is the longest in the world, as it reaches far upward into the Arctic Circle, and downward to the Cordilleras of Mexico and the Andes of South America.

If this were all that was to be said of the country that we are now looking upon, there would be no Alaska. But it has something besides mountains. It is the combination of the waters with the mountains that gives it a character that is quite different from the scenery of Switzerland and other mountain regions of the globe.

Nor is this all. It is not enough that the two greatest monuments of Almighty power—the mountains and the sea—are side by side; but it seems as if there had been a time when they were at war with each other, when volcanic eruptions burst out along the coast, rolling the burning lava into the sea, which turned back its waves to quench all this fire and flame; and that then still mightier eruptions hurled mountain masses into the deep, which, standing out of the water and in the water, became the islands that are strewn along this coast for a thousand miles. And when the war was over, then, as in all family quarrels, there had to be a "making up," and the sea, like a sister offended, yet loving and forgiving, came back, and kissed the cold rocks that had marred her face, and wrapped her arms about them, till, in the lapse of ages, they were clothed with verdure and beauty.

This is a very unscientific explanation of the Alaskan Archipelago, but it may answer till we get a better; and with this we give ourselves up to looking with all our eyes, as we come close to the shores and gaze into the face of islands, large and small, which follow one another with a disregard of order that is bewildering. Sometimes a dozen islets put their heads together like so many children in a cluster, through which it requires the most skilful navigation to make our way. Not only is the channel narrow, but it winds and twists till it forms a labyrinth from which it seems impossible to emerge. Then it is exciting to watch the man at the wheel. The great ship may be turned about with a very small helm, but the pressure on the helm must be very gentle when the mistake of a few feet would throw the bow upon the rocks. At such times the good Queen seemed to be conscious of the delicate part she had to play, and restrained her impatience, feeling her way gently, till the danger was past, when she spread her wings and moved forward majestically into the open sea.

In these twists and turns, it was not strange if we sometimes got turned about in our geography, and hardly knew the points of the compass. In such perplexity we had recourse to an old pilot, who had been for years on these waters, and knew every island and bay and glacier. Dear old "Captain George" seemed, like a benevolent school-teacher, to delight in our ignorance, as it gave him opportunity to show his knowledge, and when we were lost, he would bring out his chart and show us the precise point where we were, and how, through all our windings, we were steadily making progress towards the haven where we would be.

When we were out of danger, even though it were only imaginary, we gave a sigh of relief and turned with new zest to the study of the islands themselves, in which (if man may criticise nature) there is at first an oppressive monotony. Day by day the scene is the same—woods and waters in endless succession. In the early days of the world, when the earth was without form and void, or even when it was beginning to take shape, this coast must have had a haggard appearance, as if nature appeared with dishevelled locks, and in a blind fury, not to create, but to destroy. But when the Spirit of God moved upon the waters, they grew calm, and the savage rocks were "clothed upon" with verdure and beauty.

Looking a little more closely, I observed that every one of these islands was built up with a certain order. Beginning at the water line, the waves, in washing away the earth, reveal the rock foundation, which, as it girdles the island, seems like a sea-wall surrounding a fortress. On this immovable base rise the slopes of the hills, covered with dark evergreen foliage, whose beauty even the winter cannot hide. Each separate island has the same shape—that of a cone—and each is plumed and crested with pines. But I correct myself. What we call pines are cedar, fir, and hemlock. Pines grow farther back from the sea, and on higher ground. Sometimes the mountain tops are capped with snow. But not so often as might be supposed, for the Japanese Gulf Stream flows so near the coast as to diffuse its warmth all along these shores, so that, for the greater part of the year, these islands, though so far in the north, are "dressed in living green."

But in a ship's company as large as ours, there is always some tough old fellow who does not care for "poetry," but looks at everything in a hard, practical way, and puts a damper on our enthusiasm by asking sharply, "What is all this country good for, anyhow? It is very pretty to look at, but in all these Thousand Islands there isn't an acre that is fit for any kind of agriculture. A farmer couldn't have a garden patch big enough for a few rows of corn and potatoes."

But a country may be poor in one thing, and rich in

another. The seal fishery alone has paid all that Alaska cost us. And as to agriculture, if a man cannot raise corn, he can perhaps find wherewith to buy it. Gold has been found in some of these islands, and if the miners are not satisfied with the food supplied by "the abundance of the sea," but must have their roast beef, perhaps an exchange of the product of their mines for a boat-load of provisions from the boundless stores of Mr. Armour, in Chicago, would be agreeable to both parties.

And the forests with which these islands are wooded to the top, do they not furnish an inexhaustible supply of lumber for the purposes of commerce? Not so great as some other parts of the Pacific Coast, as, for instance, the forests on the Sierra Nevada in California, whose mighty trunks are so prized for ship timber, for masts and spars. There is, indeed, one tree grown on these islands that sometimes attains to one hundred or one hundred and fifty feet, and might well serve to make "the mast of some great admiral," were not its wood of too fine a texture, and too costly, to be set up on a ship's deck and exposed to the storms of the ocean. This is the Alaska cedar, which is one of the precious woods that is reserved chiefly for household furniture, as it has at once the hardness required to take a fine polish, a delicate color—a pale yellow—and exhales a fragrant perfume. But for timber, the trees are not of so much value after we get above Vancouver, as they are not of the same majestic stature. Those that grow on the mountain sides are but stunted specimens of what may be seen in the great forests of Washington, Oregon, and California.

But if it must be confessed that the trees of this northern climate have not the luxuriant growth of the tropics, yet the Arctic vegetation has a beauty all its own. The very mosses that cling to the rocks, and shiver in the winter wind, are exquisite in form and color; while of trees the two kinds of spruce, which grow in millions, covering rocks and hills and mountain tops with their deep green, form a rich background, from which, not unfrequently, leaps a waterfall, making a trail of living brightness down the dark mountain side. Such scenes cannot be too often repeated, and he who would complain of their repetition as "monotonous," might as well complain of the monotony of the starry heavens.

But that which impressed me most, as we sailed on and on, was the absence of life. It was a world all glorious to behold, but a world without inhabitants. Even of animal life I saw nothing. The sea itself is, indeed, full of life, but on these leafy shores I saw not even a deer peering out from under the trees. In the interior there are bears in the forests, and on the mountains, and abundance of other game; but on the islands I saw none. Still more appalling was the absence of human beings. I looked for Indians, but for days together I saw not a single canoe darting out from under the closely wooded shores. I did not even hear the dip of an oar in the distance. All was silence and solitude. It was a fresh, new world, waiting for the footsteps of future generations.

When those generations will come, we cannot tell. With all the picturesqueness and beauty of this Alaskan Archipelago, we cannot expect ever to see it the home of a large population. It may have a few hundred, or a few thousand, fishermen, who will spread their nets on the top of the rocks, like the fishermen of ancient Tyre. But may it not have a population of another kind, at least for certain months of the year? A trip to Alaska is already one of the recognized summer excursions, as much as a trip along the coast of Norway. May not these islands be the sanitarium of the North Pacific, to which thousands, worn out with labor and care, shall resort to inhale the fresh air of the sea, and grow strong again?

As the merchant princes of Boston have seized upon every point on the New England coast from Nahant to Bar Harbor, why should not the princes of the northwest build their cottages by the sea among the islands of Alaska? Here are sites as picturesque as any in the Swiss or Italian lakes. This archipelago has hundreds of Isola Bellas, that will be no less beautiful than that in Lake Maggiore, when their hillsides are terraced and dotted with villas looking out from under the shade of stately trees, with many a nook nestled in flowers and vines. In another generation it may be the fashion to have a seaside cottage in Alaska! Then it will be the resort of yachtsmen, whose launches will skim these inland waters, and glide through these narrow channels, as the gondolas glide through the canals of Venice. I can almost hear the song of the gondolier!

And why should not instruction follow in the steps of pleasure? Was not this beautiful coast scenery fore-ordained by its natural fitness, and therefore by "natural selection," for the Chautauquas of the Pacific, where the many-voiced teachers of our day may pitch their tents, and discourse of wisdom and of truth?

All this may seem the wildest fancy. But old men are permitted to dream dreams and see visions. Did the wise men of the East, who taught in the groves of the Academy, exhaust all the wisdom of the ages? In some things—as in science—the moderns know more than the ancients. And as for the great problems of life, they are the same for men of all countries and all times. So, visionary as it may be, I will indulge the hope that in the future this American Archipelago may serve for something more than for pleasure and for health, even as a place for high thoughts and generous inspirations to all who sail along these shores.

CHAPTER X

THE GLACIERS

NEXT to the wilderness of islands, and the great mountains on the coast, the wonder of Alaska is its glaciers. We had a foretaste of these on the Canadian Pacific, at Lake Louise, and in the great glacier of the Selkirks. But these were only the porticoes of the wondrous temple of ice and snow that we are now to enter. And here the ascent is gradual, from glory to glory. Even in Alaska we do not find the most stupendous glaciers till we reach Upper Alaska. It is not till we pass Fort Wrangel that we begin to open our eyes in awe and wonder.

The first thing that arrests attention is the peculiar formation of the coast line, which is corrugated with mountain ridges, between which are the fiords. The fiord is the home of the glacier; we might even say the creation of the glacier, which, by the mere force of gravity dragging it downward, and by the storms that pile up new drifts behind it, is pushed onward, till the accumulated mass cuts a deep fissure on the mountain side.

Perhaps the geologist, who would speak with scientific accuracy, would say that the glacier is not the sole creator of the fiord, nor its original "inventor," but that, before the ice and the snow began to descend in the path of destruction, there was a great catastrophe in the mountain ranges. It is a curious fact that the coast line is not straight, but curved or waving, winding in and out, as if it would follow the line of beauty; and what is still more remarkable, that it corresponds to the line of the mainland, so that they are evidently parts of one whole, and were once interlocked in a close embrace, from which they were torn apart by some eruption, but still keep in sight of each other, as if they hoped some day to come together again. A similar separation has taken place in California, only that the rocks and cliffs that have been set off, like offending children, from the mother chain, the Sierra Madre, have not been driven quite so far from house and home, but only pushed forward a certain distance, to form a lower range, a sort of advance guard for the snow-clad mountains behind; while a thousand miles farther north, these ejected members of the great family of mountains are literally thrown out to sea, so that the foot-hills of California become the islands of Alaska.

But enough of science; let us take our seats on deck, under the awning, and look for ourselves. This is a red letter day, for as we sail northward, glacier after glacier unveils its glittering form as it shines so brightly on the dark background of the mountains. And now we turn into Taku Inlet, on a little matter of domestic economy, to take in a supply of ice for the ship. The bay is full of fragments of the mighty glacier that glistens miles away at the end of the fiord. Within a few rods of the Queen there is enough of floating ice to supply the British navy. Look how the sailors fish for it! They catch the berg in a net; but the net must be large and strong. It is made of the stoutest cordage, and when it is cast into the sea, with the skill of fishermen they draw it around some ice-floe, which in an instant is hauled up, as they would haul in a monster fish, and once on deck, is put under the axe, and cut up into blocks, to be stowed away in the bunkers below. It was a novel experience to feed on icebergs; to have a glacier as an attachment to the culinary department, serving us with a necessity of our daily food, not by the pound, but by the ton!

As we resume our course, these observations of nature are interrupted by seeing in the distance a town, which, though we should not count it as much more than a village, is the largest town in Alaska. This is Juneau, so called from a Frenchman who had the good luck to find gold in this vicinity. The greatest thing it has to show, in proof of what treasures may yet be found in the earth, is the Treadwell Mine, a mile or two from the town, where, though the ore is of a low grade, yielding only from three to nine dollars a ton, yet the amount of ore is so great, and the cost of reducing it by the improved processes so small, that the product is sixty thousand dollars a month! The stamping mill by which the rough ore is ground to powder is the largest in the world! So they say, and so I believe, having tramped through it; and as to the energy with which it is worked, I can testify that it is a veritable Vulcan's Cave, with its two hundred and forty "stamps," resounding like so many trip-hammers that never cease their clang. The manager told me that for some months it had stopped *but once* (and then only for a few minutes), running day and night, weekdays and Sundays!

Of course, where there is gold, or even the possibility of finding it, thither will flock all sorts of adventurers; and, as Juneau is the point from which they set out on their voyages of discovery, its business is largely that of furnishing supplies for the outfit of the miner's camp: tents and tools, shovels and pickaxes, powder and dynamite, with fishing tackle for the rivers, and guns for game, or to protect himself, if perchance he should meet with bears or wolves, or with robbers, more merciless than wild beasts.

What long journeys start from this point! Here is a party that is bound for the Yukon River, hundreds of miles away, to reach which, they must climb mountains, and cross rivers, without bridges or boats, and then take their long and trackless way over a country without roads, and almost without inhabitants. No wonder that many, worn out with the long journey, sink down in despair, and leave their bones in the wilderness. Yet a thousand failures will not prevent others making the attempt, to share the same fate.

But what cannot be done now will come in time. The Yukon River is one of the great rivers of the world. Eighteen hundred miles long, and a mile wide six hundred miles from its mouth, it would furnish a commerce like that of the Amazon, but for the rigor of the climate, which closes it to navigation the greater part of the year. Here is the fatal drawback to the interior of Alaska. Though this North American Amazon drains hundreds of thousands of square miles, it is not possible to keep upon it a fleet of steamers, so long as it flows so near the Arctic circle that it is covered with ice a large part of the year.

As we go northward the days grow longer, till there is little of the twenty-four hours left for the shadows of the night. The bells have just struck ten o'clock, and I am writing on deck by daylight and might write for an hour longer. The sun has gone down, but the heavens

BAY OF CHILCAT.

are still full of light; there is a glow on earth and sea and sky, and, as to follow the windings of the archipelago, we have turned to the west, we seem to be sailing right into the sunset; while on the other quarter, the moon, half to the full, hangs low over the crest of a mountain—one of a long line of peaks white with snow —where she keeps her head down near to the horizon, as if in modest deference to the great luminary.

The day after we left Juneau, we steamed into the Bay of Chilcat, where two inlets lead up into the mainland, around which circle the mountains and the forests, in whose dark bosoms are counted no less than nineteen glaciers! But I had eyes only for one, the "Davidson," which, if I were to distinguish it from other glaciers, I should say was more beautiful than terrible, as it descends by a gentle slope from the mountain height, spreading out its fan-like borders till it is three miles wide at the shore, where it dips its cold feet in the sea. Here we reach our most northern latitude—that of fifty-nine degrees, ten minutes—from which it would take but a few degrees farther to bring us to the Land of the Midnight Sun.

CHAPTER XI

THE MUIR GLACIER

The excursion to Alaska is well arranged in its beginning and its ending. The wonderland unrolls like a panorama—scene after scene in a natural order—with a gradual *crescendo* till we are among the glaciers, the greatest wonder of all. And even here all are not of one pattern, or of the same dimensions, but there is a gradual climbing up higher and higher, till we come face to face with the most resplendent vision, which has been fitly reserved to the last.

We parted with our readers at midnight, when we were lingering on the deck as in a dream. Hardly had we gone below before the Queen was in motion; and in the silence of the night dropped down and out of one channel, and, rounding a point, entered another channel which led up to Glacier Bay, where we awoke to find ourselves at anchor. That dropping of the anchor was significant. It meant that there was something which could not be "passed in the night," nor in the daytime either, without a pause sufficiently prolonged to give us a steady gaze. What it was there could be no mistake, as we came up the gangway and saw before us a long cliff, like the Palisades, only that it was white, which we recognized instantly as the Muir Glacier, the one object that we had cared to look upon more than any other in

Alaska; that we had crossed the continent to see; and that now rose before us in the clear light of that summer morning as the crown and consummation of our journey.

But great expectations sometimes lead to great disappointments. Such is the experience of many, perhaps of most, persons on their first sight of Niagara. I take Niagara for a comparison, because there is at the first glance a certain resemblance between the glacier and the cataract—a likeness in shape and form and color, as in the elements of which they are composed. Only in the one the waters are let loose, and in the other they are held fast. The Muir Glacier is only a frozen Niagara. One must get his eye accustomed to it before he can take it all in. It is not like any other glacier that we have seen—as, for instance, the Davidson Glacier that we saw yesterday, which was a gentle creature, lying flat on its face, as if it were too modest to hold up its head, creeping and crawling, as it were, on all fours, and without a sound of anything breaking in its passage to the sea; while the Muir Glacier stands up boldly, with head erect and open face, as if it had taken its position that men, looking upon it, might behold as in a glass the glory of the Lord.

But the first impression is one of disappointment; it is not quite so grand as we had expected. Well, let us come a little closer to make a better observation. The Queen has steamed up to a position almost under it, as the little steamer at Niagara comes up so close that it sometimes catches the drifting spray of the waterfall. But it takes good care not to come within even the outer verge of the waterfall itself, lest it be sent away whirling like a top, if it do not share the fate of some hapless boat that has been caught in the rapids above, and gone over only to appear in the broken fragments that emerge in the whirlpool below. So our good, faithful Queen, which we have so far not trusted in vain, takes good care to keep well beyond the danger line, lest a little eagerness to see too much should bring her within the sweep of one of those icy columns that is toppling to its fall, carrying the weight of a hundred tons, that would break deck and hull, and put an end to her proud career on the sea. But there is no need of any exposure to danger. At the distance of two hundred yards we can see distinctly, and look all along the line of the outer wall and take our measurements.

"The glacier is not so high as we expected!" Indeed! and what did you expect? That it would tower into the clouds? Or will you be content to have it as high as Niagara? Well, it is a good deal higher. Niagara is a hundred and fifty feet high; the Muir Glacier is *two hundred and fifty feet!* But that is not the full measure of its greatness. Those who have studied glaciers tell us that one thus projected into the sea has at least twice, if not three times, as much of its bulk below the surface as above it. Our Captain Carroll himself once made soundings here, and found that the glacier touched bottom at a depth of seven hundred and twenty feet! If, then, some tidal wave should rush into Glacier Bay, and rush back again, so as to leave the bottom for an hour or two bare to the sun, those who should look upon it would be face to face with a sea-wall more than a mile long and nearly a thousand feet high!

So far we are observing from the outside. We are but lookers-on in Venice. But we need not stand afar off to make our reverence. Not only can we enter the presence of the Ice-king, can we confront him to his face and look him in the eye; but we can go ashore and come up close to his royal presence; and, treating him as we would Saint Nicholas, may pinch his icy beard, and even climb upon his back, and, as conceited mortals are apt to do, trample him under our feet. As soon as breakfast is over, the boats are brought to the ship's side, and gay parties, full of excitement, put off for the shore. Landing on a sandy beach, it seemed ridiculous to come upon a man playing the part of a Swiss guide in offering us alpenstocks! Of what use could they be to us gay revellers, who were but taking a morning promenade on a plank walk? Before we got back, however, we found something besides the plank walk, and were glad enough to steady ourselves by striking the sharp iron into the glittering but treacherous ice which is seamed with crevasses, that are so many pitfalls under our feet. But first we took the glacier, as we would take a fortress, in flank, walking over the broken ground, gradually approaching nearer and nearer, till, after perhaps a mile, we came alongside the huge creature, and stepped bravely upon his back. He did not resent the indignity, but seemed to tell us to make ourselves at home, an invitation which, as in some other cases, it is prudent to take with limitations. But at first we were quite as much at ease as if we were enjoying a winter scene in New England. Before us was a boundless snow-field, where the winds had been at play, tossing up the snow into a thousand fantastic shapes. Ice is a trifle harder than snow, but in its formation it lends itself to every wild fancy of the waters or the winds. As long as we had a clear field before us, we trudged away with not a thought of danger. But presently the surface grew more uneven. Wherever the wind had swept over the glacier as the rain or the snow fell, it blew them hither and thither, forming hillocks, from which the elements smoothed off any projecting points, so that the whole ice-field was in hummocks, which, while they were so rounded as to answer to all the lines of beauty, had a cold, glassy, unsympathetic look that lured us on, but gave no promise of safety. A vague impression began to creep over me that walking on a glacier was not quite like walking in Broadway. The impression was not altogether alluring, and, in spite of all our bravery of an hour before, when we set out on our promenade, I began to feel that I might as well step gingerly over the bald head of this Ancient of Days, who might, if we should take too great liberties, put us out of sight in one of the crevasses that yawned beneath us like so many icy sepulchres, and was not a little relieved when I could bow myself out of his venerable presence.*

Once clear of the ice, we strode on with a feeling of safety, though the *moraine* which borders the glacier is covered with the débris of rock, which makes it anything but easy walking, especially as we left what is called by courtesy the path, and struck off to the right, clambering over stones and almost sliding down the soft places, that we might land somewhere nearer to the foot of the glacier, which is such a giant mass that it not only cuts a deep gorge into the sea, but spreads out broad wings on either side, so that we could walk for some distance right in front of these icy cliffs as if we were on the sands

---

* It seemed to me then, and seems to me now, a great risk to let these **parties** go in such **numbers** without being attended, **as in** Switzerland, by guides, **strong, sure-footed, of** cool head, **with** alpenstocks and ropes in case of extreme danger.

under the cliffs of Dover! And now look up! How high those pinnacles tower above us! It would take a cooler head than mine to stand, even for a moment, on that giddy height, and look down at the depth below.

And underneath, what caverns there are cut out by the waters rushing through them, leaving above a vault of clear blue ice, so cold and pitiless! And the river itself, which comes forth out of the darkness, and rushes so madly over the sands in its haste to plunge into the sea, will not this very fury exhaust itself? How long will the glacier keep it going? Will not a few hot summers melt this mountain of ice and snow, so that the river will leave only an empty bed?

So small is our range of vision, that we should limit the forces of nature, or the time which it may command to do its work! The fountains that feed this river are not all shut within the circuit of these hills. The glacier has a hundred arms that reach far up into the mountains, down which the waters flow. Fed from such sources, the stream that rushes so fiercely from the foot of the glacier began its race hundreds of years before we were born, and will continue to run hundreds of years after we are in our graves!

I came back to the ship with a great respect for the Muir Glacier as not all a dream, but a substantial reality, which had a right to be in this world, and was not to be approached lightly or unadvisedly. In spite of the disappointment of the first impression, it now rose to the height of my expectations. Indeed, it surpassed them; in the mere matter of dimensions it was larger every way, longer and broader, higher and deeper. Nor was it lifeless and motionless, lying prone upon the earth, an inert mass, imbedded in a hollow of the mountains; it was a body in motion, as if it were a chariot on wheels, never resting, never ceasing in its march, with its cold eye fixed like the eye of death, pushing on day and night, crushing everything in its path, as if its mission on earth were simply to destroy.

And here we are face to face with this grim destroyer. Have we any way to stop him in his course? Has he not given us proof already of his power to bear down all resistance? The glacier is at once the remnant and the reminder of the Ice Age of prehistoric times, when great seas were frozen into solid ice, that swept over continents, carrying away whole mountain tops, and transporting enormous boulders hundreds of miles, to be imbedded in plains and valleys, there to remain to the end of the world, the monuments of its tremendous power.

This we look upon as the work of the past. But have we considered that the ice and the snow still keep dominion over a considerable part of the habitable globe? The very name of the Himalayas—that great mountain mass that rises up in the heart of Asia—signifies the Abode of Snow, an abode from which it cannot be dislodged by all the power of man, nor even by the forces of nature itself. The fiery sun of India, that blasts the plains watered by the Ganges, cannot make the smallest impression on those awful heights and depths that have been accumulating from century to century on that "roof of the world." There they remain, as enduring as the mountains themselves, perhaps to be dissolved at last only by the final conflagration, in which the elements shall melt with fervent heat.

Even in these milder exhibitions that we have on our northwestern coast, those who watch the growth of

MUIR GLACIER.

glaciers, and their steady march, are in doubt which of the two elements of nature is the more destructive, frost or fire. Of course, the latter is the more demonstrative when it flames out in the volcano, or the earthquake tears the globe asunder. But the snow falls silently, and the snow-field lies low. But while these feathery particles fall lightly they fall unceasingly, and the snow-bank keeps growing, growing, growing, with every storm that sweeps through the air, and every rain that freezes as it falls, till the mighty accumulation presses upon the earth with the weight of mountains, though not, like them, "standing fast," but ever in motion, day and night, summer and winter, pushing on its terrible way. Such is the power in yonder cliff that presents its cold, icy front, pitiless as death, to the human creatures that stand off at a respectful distance.

It was a moment of intense excitement when some peak was seen to waver. At first its base seemed to be crushed and crumbled, and came down like a snow-slide, and then there was a flash of something bright, as the ice caught the rays of the sun, followed by a muffled sound, and a mass of foam and spray thrown into the air. The larger bergs were broken as they struck the water, and the wreck was scattered far and wide. Many pieces were floating round the ship, while others were stranded on the beach, till the rising tide should sweep them away. As the glacier advances at the rate of five feet a day, it pushes forward hundreds of tons every twenty-four hours to a point where many a ledge hangs over the sea, and many a pinnacle, high in air, topples over and falls with a crash—a dull, heavy plunge. As the falls come every few minutes, the explosions follow one another at intervals, like the booming of guns. This did not quite satisfy all on board, who were looking for a sort of broadside from the glacier battery. I suppose we might have "drawn its fire" by firing ourselves. Many years ago I crossed the Wengern Alp, that stands over against the Jungfrau, from which they watch for the avalanches, and found that they had a way of bringing one down by firing a cannon, the concussion of which started a mass of snow from the top of the mountain, that "swung low with sullen roar" as it fell into the gorge below. In this way we might have startled an iceberg, or possibly two or three. But this might have given us too much of a good thing, for it is not always quite safe to have icebergs about a ship, as they may knock a hole in her bottom. For my part, I do not care so much for explosions as for the solemn beauty of this wondrous vision. How those icy pinnacles must glow in the light of sunset, when the white walls, rising up against the sky, shine like the heavenly battlements!

To see the Muir Glacier is an event in one's life, like seeing St. Peter's at Rome, or the Taj in India. It is a sight which does not fade in the distance. Go where he may, still is he

"By the vision splendid
On his way attended,"

till his eyes close on all things earthly, and open on the purer light of heaven.

CHAPTER XII

NATURE AND MAN FARTHER NORTH

THE Muir Glacier is the culmination of the journey to Alaska. But when we have seen it we have not seen the whole of this wonderland. We have merely passed through the Thousand Islands that form what is called the Alexander Archipelago. But outside of all this is another Alaska, which we leave behind us, not without sore regrets; and as we sail away we keep looking back towards that which would have made complete the most delightful summer excursion in the world.

If I could revise the excursion to Alaska, I would extend it at least two or three days. If, instead of turning abruptly on our course, we could pass out through one of the channels between the islands into the open sea, and take another day's sail to the north, we should come upon a coast-line far bolder than we have yet looked upon, inasmuch as it has no foreground of islands to divert the eye from the majestic background of mountains. If in some prehistoric age there were islands here, they have sunk into the sea, and the mountains themselves have come to the front, where they not only touch the clouds with their summits, but plant their foundations in the mighty waters. We can see them afar off. Even a hundred miles away we catch the first sight of the Mont Blanc of the Pacific, a far grander object than the Mont Blanc to which we look up from the Vale of Chamouni. *That* is less than sixteen thousand feet high, while our American Mont Blanc, fitly named Saint Elias from the white-haired Hebrew prophet, soars more than half a mile nearer to the sky.

Nor is it mere altitude that gives it such majesty; it has a more resplendent "diadem of snow." Mont Blanc has been often ascended. Good mountain climbers, attended by guides, make the ascent every summer; but the head of Saint Elias, I believe, has never yet been profaned by a human foot! Only last summer a party set out to attempt what had not been done before, but a member of it told me that they camped at its base two months, and made innumerable attempts without success, from the fact that such masses of snow rested, not only on its "bald, awful head," but far down its sides, for the snow line is thousands of feet nearer to the earth than the snow line of Mont Blanc. Thus the greatest of the mountains on this western coast is married to the greatest of the oceans, a combination of mountain and sea that gives a superiority to the scenery of Alaska over that of Switzerland itself, since Alaska has its Alps which overtop Mont Blanc and the Matterhorn, with the Pacific Ocean thrown in!

Nor does Mount Elias stand alone in solitary greatness. The whole coast-line of Northern Alaska has a boldness such as can be seen nowhere else except in the Andes of South America.

Nor is it mountains only, nor even mountain and seas together, that give such a fascination to Northern Alaska. As one goes farther north he comes into the Arctic circle, where, for a few weeks in midsummer, the sun does not go down, and there is no night! True, in midwinter

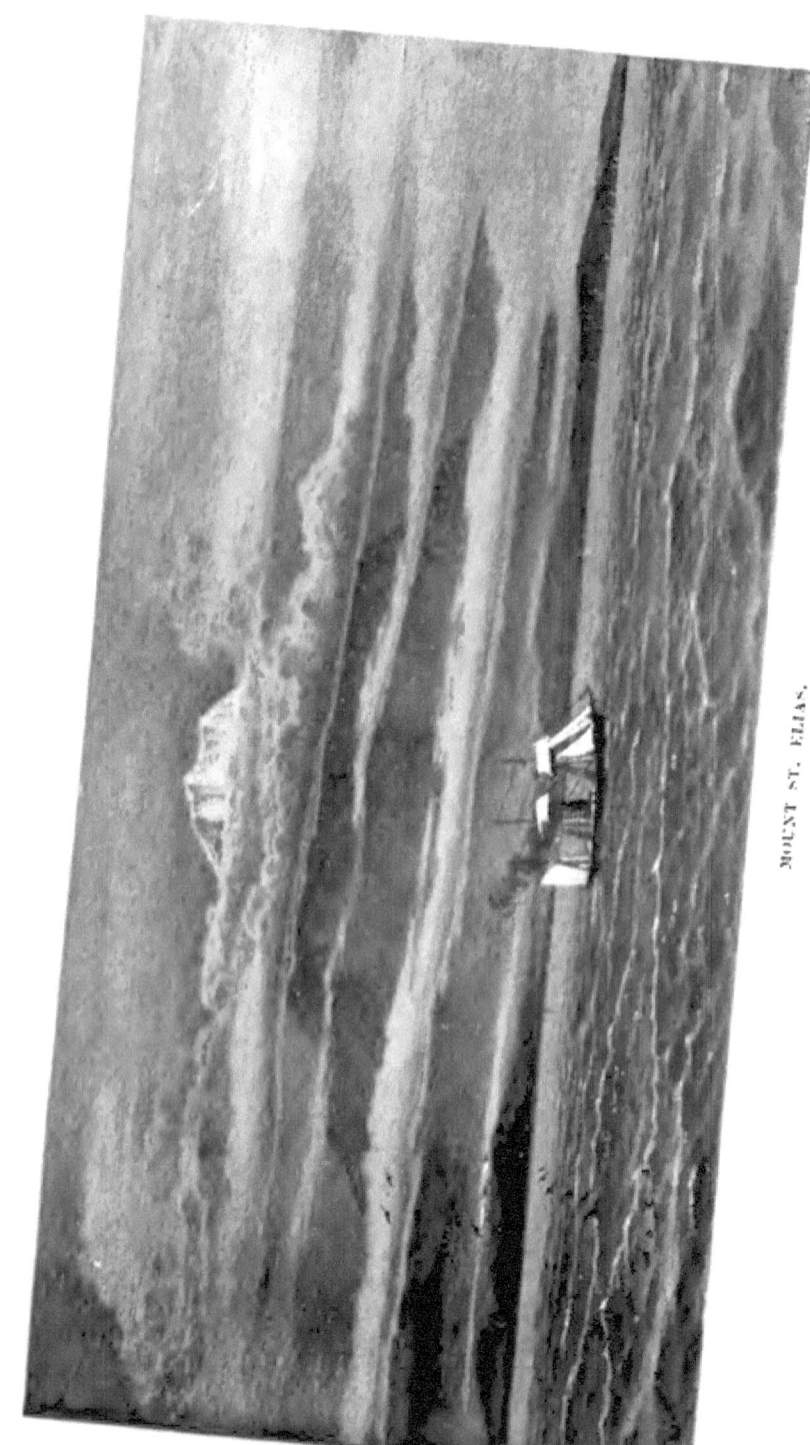

MOUNT ST. ELIAS.

all this is reversed, and there is no day. But even the darkened hemisphere has its attractions for the scientific observer. General Greely spent two winters making observations for the Government, so far north that for four and a half months he did not see the sun. But when the night was longest and darkest, the stars shone as nowhere else, while the auroras streamed up the heavens, and lighted up the Arctic night with ineffable splendors.

Added to all this, there is a human interest in these Arctic regions. Cold and desolate as they are, they are not uninhabited, and philosophers who tell us that the proper study of mankind is man may feel a scientific curiosity in inspecting this division of the race. It is a new variety of the human species, which may at least serve as a study in anthropology.

It must be confessed, to judge from the specimens presented to us, that they are not attractive, as they seem to be stunted in their growth—squat in figure, short-bodied, short-legged, and low-browed, and at the first look present no signs of physical or mental activity. Yet those who have lived among them say that they are not wanting in natural intelligence, and that if you look sharply into the little round holes in their fur caps you may see a light in their eyes, which shows that there is something in the brain behind it, possibly in the heart also, to whomsoever has the skill to penetrate this outward enclosure.

We judge of races a good deal from the way that they live, and cannot expect much from a people that live underground—that burrow in the earth. This is from a double necessity, as they have no wood to build houses, except the driftwood thrown upon their shores; and if they had, no boards or timbers could keep out the biting frost, and they must take refuge in the earth to keep themselves alive. Remembering this, you must not expect to see a New England village in the Arctic circle.

If you were to approach one of their little settlements, you would hardly see any sign of habitation, or receive any salute except from the barking of a dog. The Esquimaux dogs, which have in them a mixture of wolfish blood, are rather of the snapping-turtle order. Indeed, what may be called a village has hardly as much visible presence as a cluster of Indian wigwams. The only signs that appear above ground might be a row of scarecrows, or corn-cribs, in which to stow away what we should put in a cellar. The explanation is, that in the Esquimaux architecture the house is turned upside down, so that the cellars are raised in the air, while the people live underground, as the only place where they can lie down and keep from perishing with cold. The place is so silent that you think the people all dead, but if you will but come to where they are, you will find that they are not only alive, but very much alive. If you have the courage to let yourself down into a hole like a well, and then get down on all fours and crawl along an underground passage, you may come to a place where you can stand upright, and, when you get your eye accustomed to the darkness, see a few figures standing or sitting on the ground. There is no light except that which comes faintly through an aperture at the top, over which is stretched a piece of skin like a drum-head, through which a feeble ray trickles down into the cavern. The natives also, by dipping a bunch of dried moss in oil, make a rude lamp, which casts a faint light round a little circle. This is the Esquimaux home! In this underground cellar may be twenty people—young and old, boys and girls, babies and grannies—all crowded together in one mass of humanity!

It is a dreary picture, and yet here in this subterranean abode life goes on, and is not without its pleasures. One who has been often entertained there tells me that he has never seen a happier people. They are like children, and have the enjoyment of children, always laughing and making merry. They are very fond of practical jokes, which they play upon one another, and then burst into peals of laughter.

And they are kindly in their dispositions, and given to hospitality. If you are their guest they will set before you the best they have. "If you doubt it," said my informant, "come with me in a voyage to the Arctic regions, and I will take you to an Esquimaux home, where, if they cannot prepare you a meal after your Eastern style, they will give you a repast such as you never had before. Of course, it will not be cooked, for in most of the little settlements they rarely cook anything; they have not a stick of wood to make a fire to boil a pot, or roast a steak. But if you accept their hospitality, you must eat what is set before you, asking no questions for conscience sake. If you shrink from taking your food raw, as being a little too much in the state in which wild beasts take their food, tearing it to pieces and sucking the blood that flows from it, you may be partly relieved by the fact that 'blubber'—which is their staple of food—does not stream with blood; and that it has been frozen, which has, in a slight degree, the effect of cooking to disintegrate the fibre; and they will give you the best piece of blubber they have! But still, after all, it is rather fresh, and I dare say you will make a wry face over it; but never mind, down with it, and if it sticks in your throat, wash it down with something better than flowing goblets of German beer, viz.: pints—or quarts—of train oil!!"

This was an attractive bill of fare, to which I could only reply that I would take it into respectful consideration.

But there is a tragical side to all this, in the fact that with the limited supplies of food the natives are at times in danger of dying by starvation! In the Arctic circle the earth yields no food for the service of man; there is no such thing as agriculture; they can neither sow nor reap nor gather into barns; all their subsistence must come from the sea. They live almost wholly on the blubber of the whale and the walrus, which not long since were being rapidly exterminated. The whale fishery was not pursued for the oil, which had been almost driven out of the market by petroleum. But there was one thing that petroleum did not supply—*whalebone!* This would seem to be of small value, but we are told that the bone taken from the mouth of a good-sized whale sells for eight or ten thousand dollars—sometimes for much more! That secured, the carcass is left to its fate, what remains of it, which may not be much, since it is not as in the days when the whale was pursued in a small boat and speared with a harpoon; whereas now he can be shot from a howitzer on a ship's deck, that sends a bomb into his body, where it explodes and tears him to pieces, when the fragments of his huge bulk float away, to be seized by all the devourers of the sea.

Neither is it necessary to spear the walrus (which is hunted for its ivory); it is shot from a ship's deck with a repeating rifle that can dispose of a whole herd in a few minutes, when the tusks are torn from the bodies, which are left to drift away upon the waves. Thus the sea hunt becomes a war of extermination of this mighty game, which may be a happy despatch for the hunters, but is death to those from whom this ruthless slaughter takes away the means of subsistence. Such was the condition of the Esquimaux in the summer of 1890.

Where was relief to come from? Not from the whalers, who were carrying on a war of extermination of the whale and the walrus, their only means of subsistence. Civilization did nothing for them. It only robbed them of their food and left them to starve. And, as if that were not enough, it sometimes hastened their extermination by introducing among them the thirst for fiery drinks and other vices of civilization. There were rovers of the sea, who were little better than pirates in keeping up a secret and contraband trade in ardent spirits, in which they debauched the natives and robbed them of their furs—the only thing they had to sell—in exchange for rum, which destroyed both body and soul. The result was sometimes one of indescribable horror. One summer a revenue cutter sailing north touched at the lower end of St. Lawrence Island, and the sailors went on shore to revisit a group of villages which they had left the year before with six hundred inhabitants. But as they approached the spot they were appalled at the mysterious silence. They came to the little huts and passages to the underground habitations in which the people had burrowed, but not a sign of life appeared. As they pushed their way into the dark interiors they found the late inhabitants silent in death. As the Arctic cold had preserved the bodies from decay, the forms were still there, stretched upon the cold earth, or doubled up in some shape that showed how they had writhed in agony. The glassy eyes were "all wide," as if they glared at the intruders upon the place of the dead. Mouths were open, as if hungry for the food which did not come, and hands clenched as if grasping for some last hope before they were frozen in death. It was an Arctic Pompeii, where gaunt hunger had done what the ashes of Vesuvius had done in another age and another part of the world.

Of course, there was a possibility of accounting for this universal destruction by the breaking out of some pestilence, which in their ignorance they did not know how to combat. But the more probable explanation seemed to be that some piratical schooner—low built and painted black, as became its horrible errand—had stolen into this harbor, and smuggled in a cargo of rum, which was left behind to do its fatal work.

After such a horrid sight, it were vain to expect the preservation of the Esquimaux from what some call the "natural laws of trade." Their rescue, if it came at all, must come from another source. What could not, or would not, be done by whalers and walrus hunters, or other traders to the Arctic regions, was done by a simple-hearted American missionary. For some years Sheldon Jackson has been the agent of the Government, as well as of the Missionary Board, to visit the stations in the far north to look after the schools, and in 1890 he visited, for the first time, Arctic Alaska in the Bear, which had just come from the coast of Siberia, on which an American ship had been wrecked several years before, and the natives had shown a kindness to the only survivor that the Government wished to acknowledge by the sending of presents that the Bear was to deliver. Here they found a people very much like those on the American coast;

with only this difference, that the Siberian Esquimaux were living in a land of plenty, where they were well fed and, of course, were hale and hearty, fat and flourishing.

What made the difference? It was all explained in one word—the reindeer, which supplied the Siberian Esquimaux with *four* distinct necessaries of Arctic life: food, as the flesh is equal to the choicest venison from the deer of our plains and forests; milk, which is rich as cream; clothing, as the fur of the reindeer is more impenetrable by cold than the much heavier bearskins; and last of all, transportation, for which the reindeer are better than horses (if horses could live in this Arctic cold, as they cannot), for a team of reindeer, harnessed to a light sledge, will easily make a hundred miles a day over the untrodden snow.

Besides, they take care of themselves; they have neither to be housed, nor blanketed, nor fed. If you build a shed for them, they will not go under it, preferring life in the open air. They even drop their young upon the snow when the temperature is thirty degrees below zero. They need neither barns nor haystacks. For food they have but to strike their sharp-pointed hoofs into the crusted snow, and underneath they find in the hidden mosses and grasses an abundance of succulent and nourishing food. Was not this a beneficent provision of nature, or rather of the Father of all men, for the preservation of life in those who dwell in the uttermost parts of the earth?

But the reindeer were in Siberia, and it was on this side of the Pacific that they were needed. It was too late that season to recross the sea. But as soon as the Bear had returned to San Francisco, and Sheldon Jackson could cross the continent, he told the pitiful story of the starving Esquimaux. But, pitiful as it was, it did not at first make much impression. It seemed a visionary project to transport a herd of reindeer from Asia to America. And, after all, the Esquimaux were so far away—a plea which is often used to quiet our troubled consciences.

But in spite of all this indifference, our brave missionary kept pegging away, and the next season returned to Siberia with a few hundred dollars, with which he purchased sixteen reindeer—eight pairs—that were transported in the Bear safely to America. It was a small beginning, but it was enough to prove the success of the experiment. The beautiful creatures needed not to be acclimated, but soon made themselves as much at home in America as they had been in Asia. This encouraged him to ask of friends at the East the means to carry out the experiment on a larger scale. The late Mr. Elliott F. Shepard contributed generously, as he did to so many other good causes, as the result of all which there are now about seven hundred reindeer, with the prospect that the herds will increase from year to year, so that in time the reindeer will spread over all Northern Alaska, and thus the first of all problems—that of how to be able to exist—will be solved.

So far, so good; and yet I heard it with a mixed feeling, for I had already solved the problem in a shorter way. No one is so wise as he who cannot speak from personal observation and experience, and I said to myself: "Wherefore is all this waste? What is the use of stocking the Arctic regions with reindeer to keep the miserable natives alive, when it would be much cheaper to bring them all away? There are but about five thousand of them all told, who could be stowed in half a dozen emigrant ships and brought to a land fit for human beings to live in. It could all be done in a single summer. It would be a holiday business. How much better this than to have to bother our heads every year with some scheme to keep the Esquimaux from starving!"

When I had exploded all this wisdom upon Sheldon Jackson, he took me down in the gentlest way. He did not tell me that my pity was thrown away. Far from it, but he threw some brighter colors into the darkness of Esquimaux life, so that the picture was not one of unmixed gloom. As to transporting them to a more temperate climate, I learned that the idea was not original with me, but had occurred to many observers, all of whom had seemed to overlook the fact that it takes two to make a bargain. "Suppose," he said, "that you had your ships all ready, but that when the time came for the natives to embark they would not go! Strange as it may seem to you, they think they have the most beautiful country in the world. With all its bleakness and desolation, they love it as the Swiss love their mountains. Now and then one or two Esquimaux are brought to the United States, but how downcast and miserable they look! Our climate is intolerable to them. They pant in the heat like polar bears, and long to get back to their more 'temperate' zone! One who came here some years since was stricken with consumption, and set out to return, and every morning his first question was, 'Have you seen ice?' If he could only get a glimpse of an iceberg, he could die in peace. A people who have such a home feeling are entitled to respect, and we shall not quarrel with them if they prefer their freedom in the land of ice and snow to our fine cities, with all the blessings—and the curses—of civilization."

I am not so bold as to say that in the diet of the Esquimaux, venison will ever take the place of their favorite blubber. Nor is the latter by any means to be despised. Soberly, gentlemen explorers of the Arctic circle, do not turn up your noses at the food of the Esquimaux. If you set out for the North Pole, before you get there you will find that this blubber, which sticks in your throats, is not only all you can get, but the only food by which you can exist. The huge mass of blubber and train oil that the Esquimaux takes into his capacious stomach is so much phosphorus that generates intense heat; it is a fire in his bones, that, with the reindeer garments that incase him, fit him to bear the intensest cold of the Polar regions.

Let him keep his blubber, and may his mouth never water for the want of it! With this, and the introduction of the reindeer, the Esquimaux are not likely to become extinct from famine. And I am proud that this deliverance from an imminent danger was due, not to any civilizer or reformer, nor even to the United States Government, but to the sagacity and humanity of a brave and true-hearted missionary.

With such protection against the rigid climate, it is not the physical conditions, hard as they are, that press most upon the life of the Esquimaux, but the fact that they are under the spell of superstitions which prompt them to the most extreme inhumanity and cruelty. They are believers in witchcraft, and ascribe any sickness or pain to an evil spirit, that must be exorcised, even if it be by murder. Hence, no sooner is one taken ill, than he or she, be it the poor old father or mother, when most in need of tender care, is dragged out of the little home into some out-house where he or she will soon perish by cold. Sometimes the parents are put to death by their children. Not that the latter are by disposition cruel, or wanting in natural affection. On the contrary, their government is patriarchal, and educates them, so far as they can have any education, in respect for parents. But life is so hard, that when the vigor of youth and manhood is gone, the aged may well feel that existence is a burden, and wish it to be put to an end. Indeed, it is not uncommon in Arctic Alaska for the old folks to beg to be relieved of their misery. Dr. Jackson tells me of a case in St. Lawrence Island, in which an aged grandmother had for two years implored her children to release her from suffering, and they finally complied, as if it were a tribute of affection, dressing her up in her finery, as if to celebrate her birthday, when all put on their best as for a domestic festival, and, gathering round her, with a cord twisted round her neck, put an end to her weary existence!

Such are the pictures of Esquimaux life! The wants of such a people are manifold. They need the commonest necessities; even so little a thing as lucifer matches would furnish the means of light in their dark, underground habitations. But they need something more than these little conveniences of civilization to give light and life to an existence that is so dark and dreary.

In the Arctic circle for a part of the year they see not the light of the sun. But his absence is partly compensated by the increased brilliancy given to the constellations of the Northern Hemisphere, which is all aglow with celestial fires. Dr. Kane used to say, that the most overpowering spectacle in nature is that of the Arctic night. And yet that midnight splendor shines down on one of the most ignorant and degraded populations of the globe; so little can nature alone do for the elevation of man. What those poor people need is not dazzling displays, but "the benefits of knowledge and the blessings of religion," which would be a sort of spiritual aurora, lighting up, not only the heavens above, but their humble homes on earth. These three little "lamps" —faith, love, and hope—would do more to brighten their poor lives than all the stars in the Arctic sky.

CHAPTER XIII

SITKA AND THE GOVERNMENT

THE return from the north was not so full of surprises as the going up. But surprise is not the only element of pleasure. A beautiful landscape is twice beautiful when seen again. So far from being satisfied or "satiated" with Alaska, I should never weary of it, and, if it were not so far away, could take a sail among its islands every summer. But we have done pretty well for a beginning. We have not seen everything. Nor was that necessary. When a man goes to Venice he is not obliged, in order to see it, to take a gondola by the month and be rowed through every one of its hundred canals. A dozen is as good as a hundred. When he has done this he can turn into the Grand Canal as proudly as if he were a Doge of Venice going in state to marry the city to the sea.

So in Alaska the islands that one sees in going up and down are as good as a thousand; for each one tells the story of them all—of their volcanic formation; of what has been done by fire, and what by water; of their peculiar vegetation; and of all the elements that are combined in what Lord Dufferin, with the eye and the pen of an artist, describes as "the spectacle presented by its coast-line, not to be paralleled by any country in the world," in which, day after day, the voyager "threads a labyrinth of watery lanes and reaches, that wind endlessly in and out of a network of islands, promontories, and peninsulas, unruffled by the slightest swell from the adjoining ocean, and presenting at every turn an ever-shifting combination of rock, verdure, forest, glacier, and snow-capped mountains, of unrivalled grandeur and beauty."

To add to the pleasure of our experience, the weather, which is apt to be capricious, was perfect; we had not a day of rain; nor was there a shadow in the sky except as the fleecy clouds gathered round the setting sun. And the nights were almost as bright as the days, with the long, lingering twilight, upon which, near the end, rose the full moon, whose soft light seemed to quiver with tenderness as it fell on the whispering woods and the rippling waters.

This charm was prolonged when we sailed into the Bay of Sitka, with the sun shining brightly on the quaint old Russian town. Why the Russians chose it for their capital it is easy to see: because it is midway between the north and the south; and has a double entrance, opening at once to the east and the west, the archipelago and the ocean; and, more than all, has one of the most spacious and beautiful harbors on the Pacific coast. As it was midsummer the mountains were covered with dense foliage, making a beautiful setting for the flashing waters. As we swept round the harbor, we saw at once how large it was, and how beautiful withal, with its hundred islands (as there are said to be by actual count), and with the lofty head of Mount Edgecombe looking down upon it, in shape not unlike Vesuvius, as it was once a volcano, for which, as for other resemblances, the bay is often compared to that of Naples, a compari-

son which is not at all necessary to establish its title to be one of the most beautiful in the world.

But with all this beauty on land and sea, Sitka has two drawbacks. One is its long winter nights, when the sun rises at nine o'clock and sets at three! How to dispose of the other three quarters of the day, is the question. If the natives had any resource but drinking, it would not be so difficult. Iceland has the same short days, and yet its people are remarkably intelligent, which they owe in part to this very fact, that, as they cannot go abroad to work, they are shut up to books, which brighten their long winter evenings as much as their blazing fires.

Another drawback is not so easily disposed of. Sitka is said to be the rainiest place in the world outside of the tropics. It is not as cold as we might expect from its latitude. The climate is not as severe as that of New England, as the Black Current of Japan comes nearer to it than the Gulf Stream comes to our New England coast. But that warm current brings something besides " ethereal mildness "; it takes up such an amount of moisture from the vast expanse of the Pacific, that great clouds rise in the west and drift eastward, and striking against the snow-clad mountain ranges, are precipitated all along the coast. And so it rains on the slightest provocation, or on none at all. A gentleman whose home is here, told me that he kept count last year, and that of the three hundred and sixty-five days, it rained two hundred and seventy! This is paying rather dear for grand scenery, for snow-clad mountains, and glaciers and waterfalls!

But not to give the place too bad a reputation, he qualified it by adding that it was not always a downpour; that sometimes the rain distilled like the dew, or came in a gentle shower, after which the clouds broke away, and the pattering drops but cleansed the air, and were followed by delicious sunshine.

As the capital, Sitka inherits a sort of dignity from the old Russian days, though there are but small signs of imperial magnificence, such as the ruins of a stately old house, called by courtesy the "Castle," as it did the double duty of being at once a fort and the residence of the Governor; a block house, built of logs, that was put up for defence against the Indians; and a small Greek church, for the service of the few descendants of Russians, who still abide in the place once occupied by their fathers.

For a long time after Alaska came into possession of the United States, it was treated with strange neglect. The only sign of a change of sovereignty was the flag flying at Sitka and a revenue cutter lying in the harbor, whose captain was the only official who was clothed with authority over anybody, white man or Indian. He alone could arrest one who had committed a crime, and if it were robbery or murder, he might try him by a drum-head court-martial and have him shot or hung, but such a thing as a civil court, or trial by judge or jury, was wholly unknown. It was not till seventeen years had passed, in 1884, that Congress passed the organic act creating a government, adopting the laws of Oregon for the Territory, with a Governor, appointed by the President; and a Judge, a District Attorney, and a Marshal, to set up a court; four commissioners and four deputies divided between Sitka, Wrangel, Juneau, and Unalaska. Here was at least the skeleton of a government, with a slender personnel, but sufficient to set the machinery going, and to put Alaska under the reign of law. It touched our patriotic pride as we drew up to the wharf to see the stars and stripes flying, and a little parade ground opposite the landing, with half a dozen field-pieces to fire a salute on the arrival and departure of "dignities," though the military establishment is not on a war footing, the whole force consisting of forty marines detailed from the Pinta, the small naval vessel that is considered sufficient to do duty in these waters. But there may be a very good government without an armament. If the old democratic saying be true, "That is the best government which governs least," the less display of power the better. There is not much need of soldiers, except to protect the peaceable inhabitants, and to maintain justice by the prompt arrest and punishment of crime.

Alaska is fortunate in having for its Governor a good Pennsylvania Presbyterian, Mr. James Sheakley, who had a previous experience of several years as school commissioner. He was absent on the revenue cutter, looking after the affairs of the Territory, but his wife gave us a kindly welcome to their home, and his son took us about the town, the brightest spot in which is the mission school, with its Indian children learning the ways of civilization along with Christian truth; and the medical provision for the relief of the poor sick, whose ignorance makes them so helplessly wretched. From the school he led the way to a retreat in the woods, where a stream, fed by the snows from the mountains, comes out of the dark recesses of the forest to the sunshine and the sea. Along this stream is a beautiful path, opened by our soldiers soon after Sitka was transferred from Russian to American hands.

So far as I could learn, there is not much crime in Alaska—not more, at least, than is to be found in any border territory. The natives are poor and degraded, and filthy in their personal habits, but they are not the fiercest of savages. On the outskirts of Sitka is the Indian quarter, where one may see groups sitting in the sun, with ragged garments and unkempt hair, as wretched specimens of humanity as one could find in any heathen country. But there may be filth and squalor without crime. They would not break out so often in deeds of violence, were not their tempers inflamed by that which sets on fire the blood of men of all countries and all races—white, red, or black. So that the question of civilizing the Indian in Alaska, as elsewhere, depends chiefly on keeping him away from that by which he is demonized, or "set on fire of hell."

Recognizing this great danger, the laws for the prohibition of ardent spirits in Alaska are of the most stringent kind. But can they be enforced? That is the problem. It is not an easy matter to police a coast of a thousand miles, and where there are more than a thousand islands, behind which the swift canoe of the smuggler can dart beyond pursuit, and hide the forbidden spirits in the recesses of the forest.

To this the advocates of prohibition answer, "Nonsense! Let the Government give us a revenue cutter, with two or three swift launches, and we will soon run these smugglers to their holes. It is not for want of sufficient means, but of determined purpose, that the curse is suffered to remain to blight the prosperity of this far-off territory."

But even if the law could be enforced, some are still opposed to the policy of prohibition. They take a tone of pity for the poor miner, arguing that he has a right to have his little drink, and that it would be cruel to rob him of what is often the sole comfort of his hard life. Without some stimulant, they tell us, it is hardly possible to exist in this cold, harsh climate, especially for one leading a life of such privation and exposure. They draw a picture of the miner taking his pick at early morning, and starting for the mountains in search of gold. All day long he climbs the heights, or plunges into the depths. It is raw and cold; the thermometer is below zero; the rain begins to fall; or he is blinded with snow, till night comes on, and he drags himself back to his tent wet and shivering, tired in body, and sick at heart. Nothing can stir his blood and set it flowing in his veins like a good glass of hot whiskey! Would it not be the extreme of cruelty to deny the poor fellow his only comfort and only luxury, on which even his life may depend?

This is a strong plea; and it requires some courage to expose one's self to a charge of cruelty. Rather would we take the part of the Good Samaritan. But is whiskey the only resource? If the brave miner would suffer a word of kindness, might I not say to him, "Would it not be just as well for you, if, when drenched to the skin, instead of rushing to the whiskey bottle, you should kindle a blazing fire, that should send a glow to your very bones; and then put the kettle on, and make a cup of strong coffee, such as your wife would make for you at home? Would not that be equal to the best of Old Bourbon or Old Rye to warm you through and through? And if all in the mining camp should follow your example, would there not be fewer broken heads and bloody noses?"

But it is on the poor Indian that the curse of drink falls most heavily. To him it means death and extermination; and it is for that very reason that some of our countrymen look upon it with entire composure, as the shortest and most effective means of getting rid of the whole race of red men. Visitors to Alaska will often hear, on the steamer, a loud-mouthed talker, who thinks himself very wise, expatiating after this sort:

"What are we going to do with these miserable natives? They are a bad lot. Indians are not good for much anyhow. They are lazy, dirty, and shiftless. We shall have to get rid of them some way. But we need not trouble ourselves about it; only let them alone, and they will get rid of themselves. Whiskey will do the business better than fighting. We have only to let the whiskey come in freely, and in this way we shall civilize them off from the face of the earth. It is only carrying out the law of the survival of the fittest, which is the great law of nature. The Indian must go, as other feeble races have gone before him. It is the will of the Almighty;" and giving a sigh—very slight it is, and hardly perceptible—and putting his cigar to his mouth, he will puff away with a vigor that shows his entire acquiescence in the mysterious ways of Divine Providence.

There is a certain brutal frankness in this—in the avowal of a purpose of extermination of a whole race; but only a cowardly hypocrisy will in the same breath talk of Divine Providence and the survival of the fittest.

Nor is fire-water the only danger against which these poor creatures need protection. They are maddened by drink, and they are maddened by superstition, and here they need to be protected against themselves. They are believers in witchcraft as much as the natives of Darkest Africa. For whatever of disease may come upon them, they have but one explanation: somebody has bewitched them; and, in their rage and fury, which is all the greater because it is blind and unreasoning, they turn upon whomsoever their suspicion, or their hatred and malice, can suggest as the possible author of their misery; and hence sickness and suffering, which should call forth the tenderest sympathy, cause husband or wife, brother or sister, son or daughter, to flee from the sick and the dying, while the sufferer calls down curses on the suspected, and stirs up his own kindred to acts of murder. Only recently a woman who was suspected of witchcraft was seized and taken into the forest, and, with her arms tied behind her back, was bound to a tree, and left to perish. At the very moment of our visit, the medicine-man by whose instigation the deed was committed was in jail at Sitka, to be tried for his crime.

The next day I saw in the little church at Fort Wrangel two old men who escaped a similar fate only by fleeing for their lives. One had but just come in. Finding that he was an object of suspicion, he flew to his canoe and took to the water, hiding behind the islands and creeping along the shores, under the shade of the trees, till night came on, and then putting off into the stream, and rowing with all his might, he reached Fort Wrangel, where he found protection. He had hardly yet recovered from the horror of his situation, and it did me good to give him a hearty grip of the hand, and to assure him, as others did, that at last he was safe!

But much as he had suffered, he did not complain. This is one of the peculiarities of the race. The Indian is a stolid creature. Indeed, there is in him something like the Moslem fatalism and stoicism. If he suffers, he suffers silently. Even if he is to be put to death, he asks no pity from his enemies, but wraps his blanket about him with Roman dignity, and bows to his fate. This may not move us so much as the loud wailings by which weaker races appeal to our sympathy, and yet there is something in that dull, dumb silence, which commands our respect for a race that can thus "suffer and be strong."

So with the other sex: however unhappy they may be, they do not parade their griefs; they do not strive nor cry, nor lift up their voice in the streets. Nothing moves my indignation so much as the imputation upon their virtue. All over the world, where human beings are crowded together like cattle, whether it be in wigwams or in the slums of great cities, the conditions are such as to break down natural reserve and delicacy and modesty. But give to Indian girls the same retirement that we give to our own daughters, and they will not be wanting in any of the proprieties. In the Indian schools at Sitka and Juneau and Fort Wrangel one may see young maidens as modest as can be found in any seminary in New England. The little creatures are often as shy as the young deer in the forest, their eyes drooping at the look of a stranger, and their voices as soft and gentle as if they hardly dared to speak. The power which extends over them its strong arm, is the protector of this helpless childhood, and in that of the pure womanhood and strong manhood, which are the foundation of civilized society.

CHAPTER XIV

SCHOOLS AND MISSIONS

When Alaska passed from the hands of Russia into those of the United States, it might have been expected that the breath of liberty would waken all that coast to a new life, that would show itself, not only in the government, but in business and commerce, and, most of all, in the care shown for the supreme interests of education and religion. Not that our predecessors had been altogether forgetful of these interests. The Russians generally carry their religion with them, and at the very beginning of this century, in 1804, as soon as there was a government at Sitka, there was a Greek church. Nor was the exercise of religion restricted to the national church; for, forty-two years later, in 1846, the Governor —Etolin—was a Lutheran, and had a church of his own faith, composed of Russians, Finns, and natives. Indeed, ten years before the first Greek church at Sitka, one was built at Saint Paul on Kadiak Island, which has just celebrated its centennial.

But of course, when Alaska became a part of the Great Republic, we expected, or might have expected, that a "sunburst" of liberty, education, and religion would rise like one of its own auroras over all its woods and waters. But to our shame it must be confessed that, after getting possession of the country, we did not seem to know what to do with it. As I have already said, it was not till seventeen years after the "passing of title" that we gave it so much as a government. And as for religion, it is recorded that on the Sunday after the transfer in 1867, an army chaplain, Rev. Mr. Rayner, conducted a service in the English language; but apparently any impression it might produce floated away into the air, like the smoke of the guns which saluted the American flag. After that one prayer in the wilderness, the woods and waters relapsed into a silence—unless it were broken by some passing army or navy chaplain—that was undisturbed for years.

But private zeal did not wait for the slow movements of government. There was one man who had Alaska on the brain. It is hard to make a historic figure of one who is extremely modest in his appearance, and yet no history of Alaska can be written that overlooks the ubiquitous Sheldon Jackson, who was born to be a pioneer, and from early manhood felt that his post of duty was to be at the front—on the skirmish line—where the work was hardest and the danger greatest. I met him first in 1872 in Denver, where he was a frontiersman, on the lookout for opportunities, and wrote of him: "That indefatigable worker, Sheldon Jackson, is 'prospecting' around in all parts of the Territory, hunting up lost sheep on the mountains and gathering them into little churches, and sowing beside all waters." Those were the days when miners were exploring the Rocky Mountains for gold, and he was on their trail. Wherever they went he followed, always striking for the camp. If there was a stage coach he took passage till he came to the end of the road, and then, if he could hire an

Indian pony, he threw his saddle-bags over its back and jogged on till even the bridle-path came to an end, and then he went on foot; for he was determined to "get there," and he always did. Pretty soon he was a familiar figure in the camps, where his homely, hearty ways made him a welcome visitor. On a Sunday the miners would gather about him under a tree, and he would talk to them about the old home, and the old folks, who were thinking of their absent sons, in such a kindly way as to touch a soft place in their rough bosoms; and, after a few such visits, there might be the nucleus of a Sunday-school that in time would grow into a little church in the wilderness.

Nor was the range of this long-distance circuit rider confined to Colorado. As if he could never find work enough to do, he would now and then ride over the mountains into Utah, and preach to the Mormons in Salt Lake City; and then, turning sharply to the north, drop down among the miners of Montana. Thus he was a sort of bishop of the midcontinent, with a diocese that, north and south, extended from Canada to Mexico.

Meanwhile, Dr. Lindsley, of Portland, and other leaders of the Church on the coast were looking eagerly towards Alaska, on which Sheldon Jackson had long had his eye, though he did not visit it till 1877, when he opened a school at Fort Wrangel, which was put in charge of Mrs. McFarland, as noble a woman as ever devoted herself to a missionary life. He had felt from the beginning that what was needful for Alaska was to supplement and complement the court-house with the school-house. To this end Congress appropriated forty thousand dollars for education, of which twenty-five thousand were for public schools, and fifteen thousand for what are called " contract schools "—a provision which would have been of little value, if the Secretary of the Interior had not at once appointed Sheldon Jackson to take charge of the fund and see that it was faithfully administered.

To do this, and do it well, required a preparation that could not be made off-hand. The teachers must be chosen with care; they must be picked men and women. And there were other indispensables for those who were going to plant little colonies on islands that were a hundred times more desolate than that of Robinson Crusoe, for on all the Aleutian Islands there was not a single tree*—not a stick of wood to light a fire, or to build even a wigwam. All was bleak and barren, as so many rocks swept by the waves. They had therefore to take boards to build their little houses, with nails and hammers to put them together; with desks and benches for the schools, as well as primers and books; and last, but not least, some plain and coarse clothing for the children to cover their nakedness.

Thus equipped with everything needed, the schooner Leo, which the government had chartered for the purpose, sailed from Seattle in Puget Sound, in 1886, for the Aleutian Islands. The year before, Mr. Jackson had sent a teacher—who was a Jew—to Unalaska, to open a school, the first in all these islands, save, perchance, some little schools attempted by the Greek

---

* It is said that forty years before, a visitor had set out a few firs in a sheltered cove, in Unalaska, where they have had a stunted growth, but are not even now over twenty feet high. With this exception, there is not a single tree in a distance of five hundred miles!

priests whom the Russians had brought with them, and by the Alaska Commercial Company. Schools were now distributed at four other points: Unga, Kadiak, Afognak, and Klawack on the Prince of Wales Island, at each of which was left a teacher with his family.

That surely was a memorable voyage. The little schooner sailing away into the Northern seas, and passing from island to island, leaving at each "a teacher with his family," was another Mayflower, dropping the seeds of civilization in the wilderness. Of course, the school was followed by the church, and here a peculiar beauty was given to the early missions in the way that different denominations entered the field and worked together. This harmony was not a happy accident, but the result of forethought, and of a purpose so high that it lifted them all above sectarian pride and ambition. The field was so vast that it would have been impossible even to touch it at different points, except by concert of action, in which each division in the little missionary army should select its particular field of labor on the islands or the coast. This was the policy of Sheldon Jackson, in which he found a strong supporter in Dr. Henry Kendall, the Secretary of the Presbyterian Board of Home Missions, who invited the Methodists and the Baptists and the Episcopalians, represented by their Secretaries, Dr. John M. Reid, Dr. Henry M. Morehouse, and Dr. William S. Langford, to meet together and talk it over. Dr. Langford wrote that he could not be present, but joined heartily in the proposed agreement. The others came, but it was a small affair in outward appearance—only three secretaries and Sheldon Jackson—just enough to sit round a table; but this little company, meeting in an upper room, was sufficient to inaugurate a policy of peace, that, if adopted on a larger scale, would work for the benefit of all Christendom.

And now I see these four heads bending over the little table, on which Sheldon Jackson has spread out a map of Alaska. For the first time they see its tremendous proportions, as it reaches over many degrees of longitude and far up into the Arctic circle. The allotment was made in perfect harmony. As the Presbyterians had been the first to enter Southeastern Alaska, all agreed that they should retain it, untroubled by any intrusion. By the same rule the Episcopalians were to keep the valley of the Yukon, where the Church of England, following in the track of the Hudson Bay Company, had planted its missions forty years before. The island of Kadiak, with the adjoining region of Cook's Inlet, made a generous portion for the Baptist brethren; while to the Methodists were assigned the Aleutian and Shumagin Islands. The Moravians were to pitch their tents in the interior—in the valleys of the Kushokwin and the Nushkagak; while the Congregationalists mounted higher to the Cape Prince of Wales, on the American side of Bering Strait; and last of all, as nobody else would take it, the Presbyterians went to Point Barrow, in latitude seventy-one degrees and twenty-three minutes, the most northern mission station in the world! There is a little Danish church at Upernavik, in Greenland, which is higher—seventy-two degrees and forty minutes—but no mission station. Thus, in the military assignment of posts to be held, the stout-hearted Presbyterians at once led the advance, and brought up the rear in a climate where the thermometer was at times fifty degrees below zero—a situation that called for no ordinary amount of "grit and grace"!

Here was an ideal distribution of the missionary force, in which there was no sacrifice of principle, but an overflow of Christian love, which seemed to come as a baptism from on high. It was not in pride or scorn, but in the truest love, that these soldiers of the cross turned to the right and the left, at the command of their great Leader, and marched to their several positions of duty and of danger.

How wide was the separation of these brave men, may be seen from a table of distances. Starting from the Presbyterian stations in Alaska, and sailing northwest, one might espy a little Swedish church at the foot of Mount Saint Elias; but then turning southwest, he would have to sail five hundred miles before he came to the position held by the Baptists, from which to Unga, where the Methodists pitched their tents, is another stretch of from two hundred and fifty to three hundred miles. These are all island stations, while the Episcopalians, Moravians, and Congregationalists are on the coast or in the interior.

These distances are reckoned from the outside—from the circumference—whereas, if measured from centre to centre, the distance from Sitka to Kadiak is six hundred and thirty-three miles in an air line, and other stations "stand off" on the land, or into the sea, in the same majestic isolation. These magnificent distances would keep the most belligerent of men, even those who were sticklers for creeds and forms, from controversy. No man *could* "despise his brother" over such vast stretches of land and sea.

To appreciate the courage that faces such conditions,

we must consider what it means to be separated from one's kindred. It is almost equivalent to being cut off from communion with the human race. Living, as we do, in populous communities, we can hardly comprehend the awful silence and loneliness of the Arctic circle, where men are almost buried alive. Their situation is, in some respects, worse than that of exiles in Siberia, for the exiles can at least have the companionship of sorrow. But some of our missionaries are literally out of the world. They receive a mail only once a year! Months may pass without seeing a familiar face. In one case, a missionary was left alone among the Esquimaux for a whole winter. At last there came a party of natives with a dog which had been given them by an English trader; and for want of other company, the poor missionary trudged over the snow every day, as he expressed it, "to talk English with that dog!" How he must have yearned for the sight of one of his race, with whom he could speak in his own tongue wherein he was born! Add to this tie of blood that of Christian brotherhood, and how overmastering must be the longing for some fellow-being whom he could call brother, and press to his aching bosom!

Nor would he stop very long to ask to what denomination the Christian stranger belonged. In those high latitudes these little matters of sect get strangely mixed up, so that it is hard to tell "which is which." Dr. Jackson says, that, as he sailed from island to island, and saw the missionary coming down to the shore to meet him, he could not "tell them apart." Even when he came to St. Michael, sixty miles north of the mouth of the Yukon, and there met a Catholic priest, who had come from the interior a distance of two hundred and fifty miles, to get his yearly mail and his yearly supplies, he says, "My heart went out to him as a brother!" And why should it *not* go out to him? Robinson Crusoe on his island would find a brother in any human being. When two men meet on a desolate coast, and look in each other's faces, they are not apt to stand on ceremony. The tie of humanity is enough to draw them together. But here was a still stronger tie; both were working for the same end, to raise up humanity from its lowest degradation. How could a true-hearted man help honoring and loving one whose life was formed on the great example of sacrifice that was ever before him in the cross that hung upon his breast!

And here is the moral benefit of a life amid such hard conditions—that it throws men upon one another for sympathy and support, and upon Him who is the Creator and Preserver of all. In the Arctic regions man is bowed down with a sense of his own littleness and weakness and dependence upon a Higher Power. Who can look up to the splendor of the Arctic night without a feeling of awe that is akin to adoration? And if God be our Father, then all we are brethren, and common duties and common dangers should bind us together in a holy brotherhood.

I have been led to this train of reflection because I like to recall the names and deeds of those whom I love and honor. Our brave missionaries are making history for us. They are the pioneers of civilization, and if what they have done be not recognized now, it will be hereafter. When we are all dead and gone, and our Western Archipelago is no longer a wilderness; when church spires rise out of the primeval forest, and the sound of the church-going bell is heard over these woods and waters; then will the historians of that day seek among the graves of the fathers to find to whom Alaska owes its schools and churches, and no name will be held in more grateful remembrance than that of Sheldon Jackson.

CHAPTER XV

THE STORY OF METLAKAHTLA

WHILE we were so slow in establishing schools and missions in Alaska, British Columbia had many years before set us an example, which it is a duty to recognize to the honor of Christian heroism and devotion.

"The age of chivalry is gone," said Edmund Burke a hundred years ago. In the crash of the French Revolution he thought everything was going to wreck and ruin. But it was only the form, and not the reality. The essence of chivalry lies in courage and self-denial in a good cause—a readiness to sacrifice everything for the benefit of one's fellow-men, at any loss or any danger. And if anybody doubts whether this spirit of chivalry still exists on the earth, "let him listen to the story," not "of Rasselas, Prince of Abyssinia," but of a humble missionary on the western coast of North America.

Long before the world knew much of Oregon and California, British Columbia was known through the Hudson Bay Company, whose settlements were occasionally visited by English ships. Among these was Her Majesty's ship Satellite, whose captain was interested in missions, and was shocked to find a tribe of Indians who were given to cannibalism. Not that they were all cannibals, but it was practised by the Shamans (or medicine-men), or a certain class or "gang" in a tribe (other tribes had their gangs of dog-eaters) as a sort of religious rite—a sacrifice to appease the anger of their gods. Some of those who afterwards became Christians, said they had done it " to appease the Great Spirit, who demanded human flesh, and that if He did not get it through the appointed medium the whole tribe would be in danger of being devoured!"

Such was the story which this Christian captain brought back to England. Now cannibals are outlaws in all nations of the world. They are enemies of the human race, whom it is almost a duty to humanity to exterminate. But this brave captain would not think of resorting to that desperate alternative, at least until other means were exhausted; and he offered to the Church Missionary Society of London, as he was to return to this coast, to take any one who had the courage to peril his life in the effort to reclaim these savages.

The offer reached the ear of a young man from Yorkshire, who was at a college near London, William Duncan by name, who, with the ardor of youth, thought that here was an opportunity to see whether there was really any power in Christianity to subdue the worst of men, and he went to the Missionary Society and volunteered for the dangerous service. They took him at his word; not, perhaps, that they had much confidence in his heroic project, but they were willing that he should lead a forlorn hope, which few had the courage to undertake; and gave him what seemed to be a commission to death by martyrdom.

In due time the Satellite reappeared on the western coast of America; but when she arrived at Victoria, the governor of the island of Vancouver, and the officers of the Hudson Bay Company, stoutly opposed his going to

Fort Simpson, assuring him that his life would soon be taken by the Indians, and that the fort could afford him no immunity from danger. The governor and the captain almost got into a quarrel about his destination; but on his assuring the governor that he had counted the cost, and would take the risk, he gave way, and so, after being detained three months at Victoria, he was allowed to proceed to what seemed a certain sacrifice.

At Fort Simpson the Hudson Bay Company, deeming it necessary to take all precautions to protect its officials, had built a stockade thirty-two feet high, with guns placed in bastions at two corners of a square, which was manned and defended by twenty-two employés of the Company. Inside this stockade Duncan kept, or perhaps *was kept*, for a few months, for, had he exposed himself at any distance, he would have been straightway killed and eaten! As it was, he saw sights that thrilled him with horror. One day, looking over the parapet, he saw two "gangs" of savages in a melée, and, looking more closely, he saw that they had the body of a woman, which they were literally tearing to pieces, that they might devour it! At another time he saw three "gangs" eating the body of a boy who had died of consumption. If he had been an ordinary man he would have taken the next ship and returned to England, feeling that he had ventured as near to the gates of hell as it was safe to go. But he was made of other stuff, and lingered still, till, after he had learned enough of their language to be able to talk with them, he walked out of the gates and put himself in their power. Of course, he took his life in his hands, but the result showed that this boldness was the truest wisdom. By showing confidence in them, he gained their confidence in him. He disarmed them, not by force of arms, but by kindness. He would take up a pappoose in his arms so gently as to warm the poor mother's heart. Where even the men in the fort would not venture, he went unprotected. If he was weary at midday he would lie down under a tree and fall asleep, while all round him were those who had been but lately savages and cannibals. Yet not a man would touch a hair of his head. Thus little by little he won upon their affection and their gratitude—for savages, and even cannibals, are capable of both—till they began to look to him as their best friend. To be sure, he was somewhat of a mystery. They could not quite understand him, for they did not know what to think of a white man who had no wish to shoot them, or cheat them, or lie to them, or, indeed, any purpose but to do them good.

This practical exhibition of the spirit of Christ went hand in hand with preaching the Gospel. He entered into their humble life, and taught them the industries which they needed most; how to drain the land, and cultivate the soil, that they might have little garden patches. And not only had he the knowledge of an English husbandman, but he seemed to be a mechanical genius, who knew a little of everything. He put up a saw-mill, and showed the natives how to work it, so as to turn their trees into boards, and build neat little houses to take the place of their dirty wigwams. He showed them how to make wooden clogs to protect their naked feet, before they could afford to buy leather shoes; how to make ropes for their tents and their boats; to make casks and barrels for their fish. He taught the women how to sew and make shawls and blankets. Here were all the elements of civilization, to which he added the ornamentals in a brass band and a fire brigade. And to have not only the form, but the reality of a government, he had a council of natives to regulate the affairs of the town, and elders to keep an eye on religious work and the morals of the community, the entrance of which into the hearts of these poor children of the forest was made easier by having before them such an example of Christian character. They saw that he loved them, not merely because he was a kind-hearted man, but because of some spiritual influence that had taken possession of him, because a Higher Love had overflowed into his own great heart. Soon he had the nucleus of a little church, which grew and grew till it included the whole settlement and required a tabernacle, which was supplied by the willing gifts and labors of all, and in which was gathered every Sabbath day a body of Christian believers as attentive and devout as any that gathers in any village church of New England. Indeed, it seemed as if the little settlement had been formed on the model of a New England village, in which all things revolve round the two *foci* of the school-house and the meeting-house. That such a thing of beauty should blossom in the heart of the wilderness, was the wonder and amazement of all beholders. In 1876 Lord Dufferin, then Governor-General of Canada, made a visit to the northwest coast, and on his return to Victoria gave the result of his observations to the Provincial Government, in which he said:

"I have traversed the entire coast of British Columbia, from its southern extremity to Alaska. . . . I have visited Mr. Duncan's wonderful settlement at Metlakahtla, and the interesting Methodist Mission at Fort Simpson, and have thus been enabled to realize what scenes of primitive peace and innocence, of idyllic beauty, and material comfort, can be presented by the stalwart men and comely maidens of an Indian community under the wise administration of a judicious and devoted Christian missionary. I have seen the Indians in all phases of their existence, from the half-naked savage, perched, like a bird of prey, in a red blanket upon a rock, trying to catch his miserable dinner of fish, to the neat maiden in the school at Metlakahtla, as modest and as well dressed as any clergyman's daughter in an English parish. . . . Raise your thirty thousand Indians to the level Mr. Duncan has taught us they can be brought, and you will have added an enormous amount of vital power to your present strength."

For the good order of his little community Mr. Duncan laid down a few simple rules, which were so plain that all could understand them; but as there are several, the special reason for which may not be perceived by those not familiar with Indian life, they are explained in a few words in brackets:

1. Give up Indian deviltry. [Their old cannibalism and devil worship.]
2. Cease calling conjurers when sick. [The medicine-men, who among all Indian tribes are at the bottom of their superstitions and their horrible practices.]
3. Cease giving away property for display. [This seems a strange rule, but it was one of the first importance, as it was their custom to give what they called a *potlach*, a huge feast, in which they went to every extreme of gluttony and drunkenness, and ended by giving away everything they had in the world.]
4. Cease gambling.
5. Cease painting your faces.
6. Cease drinking liquor.
7. Rest on the Sabbath day.
8. Attend religious services regularly.
9. Send your children to school.
10. Be cleanly in person. ["Cleanliness is next to godliness."]
11. Be industrious. ["Satan finds some mischief still for idle hands to do."]

12. Be peaceful. [Indians in their natural state are always fighting.]

13. Be honest in trade. [Mr. Duncan's Indians are known all over Alaska as men whose word can be relied on; they are hard workers, and will take only what is their just due.]

14. Build neat houses. [A clean, decent home is one step towards living a decent life.]

15. Pay the village taxes.

Here was a model community, founded on the highest religious principles united with practical wisdom—what an old English writer calls " plain, roundabout common sense." Spiritual in its origin and its motive, it was not too ethereal for the daily round of common life. In a word, it was Christianity combined with civilization, where the two forces worked for, and not against, each other, with the result that all men dwelt together in peace and quietness, serving God and doing good to one another.

But this was a state of things too ideal to last. As the fame of this Christian colony went back to England, it seemed almost a reflection upon the National Church that so great a result should be achieved by one who was not a priest, nor even a deacon; and accordingly a bishop was sent out to give the faithful worker the benefit of his supervision. Of the man chosen for this office we know nothing; he may have been a learned scholar and a devout ecclesiastic; but it is not probable that he knew much about Indians, or was able to give instruction to one who had ventured his life among cannibals. Venerable as he might be in his episcopal robes in an English cathedral, his canonicals did not add to his influence among these children of the forest. The very fact that he assumed authority over one to whom the people had been accustomed to look up as their best friend, while it was a reflection upon the latter, did not attract the people to the former, so that between the two the influence of the mission was injured rather than helped by the new arrival. The attempt to carry out a full English ritual in the backwoods was about as striking an illustration of the want of common sense as could be imagined. The missionary humbly submitted that what was edifying in old Christian communities, might be a cause of offence to these poor natives, who were but just reclaimed from savagery. To administer the holy sacrament with wine was certainly according to the original institution, but was there not prudence to be used in passing the cup to one in whose blood it would stir up a fire that he could not resist? And further, in the administration of the sacrament the priest is accustomed, in offering the elements, to speak of those who receive them as "eating the body and drinking the blood" of our Lord; words which have a divine origin and a sacred meaning, but which these ignorant people might interpret literally as approving and commending cannibalism!

But in vain was argument wasted on the bishop; he insisted on the exact words, so that the strange spectacle was presented of the poor missionary being obliged to go among his people on week-days to explain away what the bishop had taught on Sunday. At length the situation became so intolerable that one or the other must retire. The bishop would not move, and the missionary was given to understand that if he migrated, taking his people with him, they left behind them all that they had created by the labor of years. This was a hard alternative, but the loss of their goods was nothing compared with liberty; and they were ready to make the sacrifice. In seeking a new place of refuge it was important to get beyond the British dominions, that they might not be subjected to a repetition of their sad experience. Accordingly, Mr. Duncan made a pilgrimage to Washington to ask for a new home in one of the islands which belonged to the United States, and obtained permission to occupy Annette Island, some seventy miles north. The change of site was an improvement. One who visited both says: "It is better every way than the old Metlakahtla, situated on a beautiful plateau, nearly level land extending to one thousand acres, with clean, shady beaches on three sides, which are highly appreciated by the Indians as affording facilities for launching and hauling up canoes, as well as for landing and shipping fish, wood, and other commodities. The soil is capable of cultivation, when drained and cleared. The food supply is abundant, venison, salmon, and halibut to be had almost at their very doors."

To this island of refuge, which Providence seemed to have reserved for them, the missionary removed with about a thousand of his people, leaving the bishop to preside over the remnant that remained behind.

Of course, the work of rebuilding their little Jerusalem was slow. It was a hard struggle to begin at the foundation and re-create all that had been destroyed. But willing hands make light work, and in due time rose a second Metlakahtla, more beautiful than the first, in which New England is reproduced somewhat as it was in the good old days of our fathers. Indeed, it seems to have been formed on the model of Puritan simplicity, and I will venture to say that there is not within a hundred miles of Plymouth Rock a village in which the Sabbath is more strictly observed; where there is less of drunkenness or immorality of any kind; where the people are more sober, temperate, orderly and Christian, than in this community of reclaimed savages and cannibals; and to-day Annette Island in the far north, where winter reigns over half the year, is fairer to the eye of a thoughtful observer than any island of palms in the Southern Sea, with its rich tropical vegetation.

CHAPTER XVI

PUGET SOUND—SEATTLE AND TACOMA

It would be a sad come-down for pilgrims to the Pacific if they should find an abrupt change on leaving Alaska; if the bold scenery should suddenly become flat and tame; if the mountains should sink down to hills, and at last die away, as if the soft murmurs of the sea had put to sleep the restless spirit of the volcano, and the low-lying, sandy beach should be as smooth and unbroken as the ocean in a calm. That tameness belongs more to our eastern coast, along which one may sail for a thousand miles without seeing a mountain, or seeing it only in the distance. On the Atlantic the mountains keep in the background, as if they were afraid to show their heads, or encroach upon the mighty deep, or even to look down upon it with a haughty crest. The land seems to bow down to the water, as if it humbly asked the waves to dash over it, and literally drown it in the depths of the sea.

But on the Pacific all this is reversed. It is given to the land to assert the majesty of nature. Power is enthroned on the mountain tops. Not only is a mountain chain always in sight, as one sails along the coast, but they crowd one upon another, pushing forward to the verge of the continent, presenting a mountain wall like that of the Himalayas, only that the latter runs east and west, cutting off the peninsula of India from Central Asia; while in the Western Hemisphere it spans the equator in one continuous chain from Mount Saint Elias to the Andes of South America.

And so we found that coming back from Alaska was not a descent, but only passing from glory to glory. The first cry of land—that is, of land in the United States— was at the sight of Mount Baker, with its head crowned with snow. Touching at Victoria seemed like coming home, for here we got our letters, and were again in communication with the world we had left behind. And even of Victoria itself, the second sight was better than the first, as it renewed and intensified the former impression. Victoria has the double outlook assigned to the old Greek battle plain:

> "The mountains look on Marathon,
> And Marathon looks on the sea,"

only that here the mountains and the sea are not separated, but are parts of one whole (for the mountains divide the seas and the seas divide the mountains), forming one glorious panorama that stretches all round the horizon.

From Victoria it is but an hour or two's sail across the Straits of Fuca, and, as it was just at evening, the sun, that was going down in the Pacific, lighted up the Olympic Range, as it lights up the Bernese Oberland in Switzerland.

In the evening we touched at Port Townsend, which, if it does not as yet take rank among the cities of the western coast, by reason either of its population or its wealth, has a very great prospective value for commerce, as well as a strategic importance in case of war from its position at the head of Puget Sound.

Puget Sound is a body of water which has some peculiar features. The only drawback to it as a station for ships outgoing or incoming is that it is in some places too deep for safe anchorage, a depth for which it is not easy to give the geological explanation. Possibly its bed is the crater of an extinct volcano, or was formed by some depression, like that of the Yosemite, so that the waters that flow over it have almost the depths of the ocean itself. But these decrease as you approach the shores, till the woods and the waters meet, and the gentle slope of the beach glides off into better soundings, and the forests cast their soft shadows on the tranquil deep. Here the anchors hold fast, and the ships, great or small, ride in safety. Thus protected, there will be many little ports, as well as fishing stations, all round this inland sea.

At the same time Puget Sound may serve as a rendezvous for our navy. Nature has made it easy for defence by a narrow passage, which can be sealed up so as to make it a land-locked harbor. Coming from the Straits of Fuca it is entered by what may be called its throat, which, though four miles long, is but one mile wide, and can easily be fortified so as to be impassable even for ships of war. Those who have visited Constantinople will remember the "Castles of Europe and Asia," which face each other from the two sides of the Dardanelles, to stop any ship that has not the right to pass. With the same ease could we put castles, or forts (such as now command the Narrows in New York Harbor), at the entrance to Puget Sound, to forbid trespass on our American waters.

But just now I would rather not talk of defences and

armaments. We do not need any Gibraltar in the Pacific, where we have no enemies and no rivals. Nor would it exalt my national pride to see Puget Sound barred with "Iron Gates." Rather let its gates be thrown wide open, that it may be a place of refuge for the storm-bound ships of all nations, who would seek for shelter from the perils of the sea.

But all speculations as to the future were set aside by the living present as we drew up the next morning alongside the wharf at Seattle.

Seattle! I had heard the name before, and that was the beginning and the end of my intelligence. But when I went on deck to take a first view from the water, I perceived that it was not exactly like the ports in Alaska, where the "shipping" is chiefly Indian canoes, but that it was in truth a city, and "no mean city" either, with wharves at which ships and steamers were loading and unloading, with all the signs of a busy, bustling population. Such surprises come rather frequently on this coast, and I find that the best way to get knowledge is to begin by confessing ignorance, and opening our eyes very wide to see and our ears to listen; and I frankly own up that I went ashore at Seattle knowing absolutely nothing about it but the name! And I should have come away not much wiser, or, at least, with but a partial and limited acquaintance, but for the courtesy of a gentleman whom we met on the Queen, who lives here, and who, in an hour after we touched the wharf, appeared with his carriage, drawn by spirited horses, with which he whirled us about the city in a few hours, and gave us a larger view of what it is now, and what it will be in the future, than I could have got in weeks groping about alone.

We did not need to go far to observe the way in which it is built, wherein it is in contrast with most Western cities (at least for the first years of their existence), where the streets are ill-paved, if paved at all, and lined with cheap frame houses. But Seattle is a city which "hath foundations." The streets are well paved, and, as we drove into the centre of business, we looked about with surprise at the massive public buildings, as well as the banks and stores. This solid architecture it owes to a fire, which, five years ago, laid its business quarter in ashes. At the moment it seemed as if the city had been swept out of existence, and could never rise again. But, as in the case of Chicago, what appeared to be its greatest calamity, proved its greatest blessing. The indomitable spirit of the people rose above disaster, and the city that rose out of the ashes was far more solid and far more beautiful than its predecessor. As we were about to extend our drive, in and out of the town, we had the good fortune to find Dr. Allison, and laid hold on him, and forced him to come up into the chariot and keep us company. He took us to see his own large and beautiful church, in which he fully expects to receive the General Assembly when next it holds its annual gathering on the Pacific. Seattle is a city of churches of different denominations, all of which would join heartily to welcome the great Presbyterian Sanhedrim. But when shall these things be? Not next year, nor the year after. But we may hope that it will be before this century has expired. And may we be there to see!

Nor did Dr. Allison fail to point out the site of the coming University, in which he interested a good many friends at the East a year or two since. The site is magnificent—a bold headland overlooking Puget Sound

—a position as commanding as that of Robert College on the Bosphorus, though the university has not yet taken possession. It has started modestly in a town in the interior, where its beginnings are small, but not a bit smaller than were those of Harvard and Yale; and by and by, when it takes possession of its Hill of Zion, and all its lamps of science and philosophy are "trimmed and burning," it will be a lighthouse of learning that will cast its rays far and wide along the shores of the Pacific.

But this is not the only commanding site in the surroundings of Seattle. The city is girdled with hills. This lay of the land would be the despair of road-makers who should wish to lay out a city four-square, with the streets all running at right angles, and on a level surface. And yet this very irregularity offers to architects and landscape gardeners the opportunity to produce their most beautiful effects. In this morning's drive we came abruptly on many a high place that would be a fitting site for a stately mansion, with a lookout over land and sea; with many a quiet nook nestled in the recesses of the hills, where a poet, or painter, or scholar might shut himself in from the world, as if he were in some airy nest on the shores of the Bay of Naples.

After a drive of four hours we were not sorry for a noonday rest at the Rainier House, which from the hill-top commands a view of miles up and down Puget Sound, and to the mountains on the west, where the sun goes down.

But the sun is not down yet, and our work is but half done. "When you go to Seattle," said a friend, "do not fail to see Washington Lake." But it is several miles out of town. Yet for all these difficulties a way is provided; for electric cars or cable cars are running everywhere, not only through the streets, but up hill and down dale with a swiftness that almost takes one's breath away, and in half an hour we were looking into the placid face of a sheet of water as beautiful as ever was embosomed in the hills. And when we reluctantly turned our backs upon it, it was only to take another long ride to another lake, with a grove on its border, where parties from the city camp in the shade, or skim the water in their light shells, forgetting all the hard labor, and all the folly and the sin, of this weary and wicked world.

But all things have an end; the day so rich in sights and experiences left us but an hour to finish our last view, and reach the boat for Tacoma.

It is but thirty miles from Seattle to Tacoma, so that they may be spoken of as sister cities; yet even sisters are sometimes jealous of each other, though both should be passing fair to the eye of a stranger; and, indeed, it sometimes happens that the more beautiful they are, the more jealous they are. To this strange law of contraries these two fair sisters are no exception. Of course, I am not going to take the side of either, especially when I can in all sincerity praise both. It is said that Daniel Webster, when asked which play of Shakspeare he liked the best, answered, "The one I have read last"; and such would very likely be the impression upon a stranger here: his preference, if he could have one at all, would be for that which he had seen last, and which therefore remained freshest in his memory. For my part, I can say truly:

"How happy could I be with either,
Were t'other dear charmer away."

Tacoma is more of an Eastern city, as it was started by Eastern enterprise (when it was fixed upon as the terminus of the Northern Pacific Railroad), built largely by Eastern capital, and settled by Eastern people. Its position is very much like that of Seattle, on a hillside rising in terraces one above another, along which are hundreds of beautiful homes, not very costly, as if built for show, but in excellent taste, each standing in the centre of a plot of ground, where the green lawn with flowers and shrubbery make the most beautiful setting for a home; and each commanding an outlook over land and sea as charming to the eye as any on the Hudson or along the New England coast.

The country about Tacoma is almost, if not quite, equal to Florida or California in the abundance of fruit and flowers. And all this efflorescence of beauty has been wrought by the hand of man upon land reclaimed from utter desolation. Not far from Tacoma is a strip of land —I know not of how many thousands of acres—lying along the river Yakima, which has been an alkaline desert, on which grew only sage grass. It was inhabited only by a tribe of Indians, some twelve hundred in all. But the white man came with his magic wand, like Moses with his rod, and struck the rock, and the waters gushed forth. Artesian wells brought the water to the surface, and this irrigation of the land, with the burning sun that poured down upon it, brought forth the golden growth of fruits and flowers that overflows the markets of Tacoma.

The home feeling of an Eastern visitor is increased by the sight now and then of a face which brings back the associations of other years. Such was the kindly face of Mr. S. P. Holmes, of the old firm of Bowen, Mc-

Namee & Co., in New York, who had long been its European correspondent, living for years in Paris. How long ago it was I knew him, I am afraid to tell; but now he has not only returned to America, but to its western coast, where he finds the air and the climate softer than in our rugged East. But though he has changed his skies, he has not changed his heart; he is as gentle in manner as in the old days, and gave me the same warm grasp of the hand, and took me about the town and to the environs, to show me how beautiful it all was. And then the Secretary of the Chamber of Commerce took me in hand to show me some of the public buildings. The Court-house is a structure that would be an ornament to any city, East or West. Not the least pleasant room in it was in an upper story devoted to an art school, furnished with the ancient statues, such as the Dying Gladiator, and copies of the great masters; where a dozen or twenty young ladies were busy with their pencils, but all hushed and quiet, since no one speaks above a whisper, so absorbed are they in their beautiful art.

But, with all these attractions, I found the people of Tacoma a good deal depressed. Its sudden growth gave it a great boom, from which it was now experiencing a reaction, and they were despondent, as if it would not recover from the setback in years; to which I answered: "Nonsense! Every city has its booms and its setbacks; I have seen a dozen in New York in the forty years that I have lived there. Look at Chicago! When it had the great fire, people thought it had gone up in smoke; but it rose out of its ashes, not only more beautiful, but richer and stronger than ever, till now it is the second city on the continent, and may yet be the first!"

After all these excursions were over, as the evening

came on, I sat on the broad veranda of the hotel, which looks out upon Puget Sound, and tried to sum up the impressions of the day, and think whereunto this city might grow. As we came up to the wharf the evening before, I had noticed a large steamship lying alongside, which was bound for China, whereupon I gave a peremptory judgment on the folly of such preparation for a commerce that did not exist! Commerce with China! There *is* no commerce (except in tea, and that could easily be carried in a few ships), nor, for that matter, with all Eastern Asia. When I crossed the Pacific in 1876, we sailed on and on for seventeen days, and did not see a single sail till just as we were entering the Golden Gate! Since then there has sprung up a little trade with Japan, but chiefly in knicknacks and lacquer ware! "What do you want of ships," I asked almost indignantly, "when you have nothing to buy and nothing to sell? Is it that you want to throw away your money? Well, the Pacific Ocean is big enough to hold it all, where your wealth will be literally drowned in the depths of the sea!"

After this explosion, I must confess that I felt rather cheap when the Secretary of the Chamber of Commerce answered mildly that there had sprung up a great trade on the Pacific, in which there was now an exchange of products, and that, instead of being merely importers, we were now exporters; that instead of these great ships going empty, "they could not carry the freights that were pressed upon them." "And what do you export?" I asked. "Wheat!" That was a revelation. Wheat is a new diet for John Chinaman. When I was in his country, he did not even know the taste. If you had seen, as I have in the shops of Canton, half a dozen men sitting round one small table, plying their chopsticks in a single bowl that answered for all, you would see that rice, and not bread, is the staff of life. But now at last poor John Chinaman is to have a "square meal" of American bread! That does not seem to be saying much, but it is saying a great deal. Good food is the first condition of good health, and good health tends to good morals. Now that this export has begun, it is not likely to be stopped even by war; indeed, the demand may be increased; and with this improved physical condition, with better food to eat, there may be a general "betterment" in manners and morals; in brighter and happier homes; so that at last we may say for poor old China that the kingdom of heaven draweth nigh!

CHAPTER XVII

THE STATE OF WASHINGTON

I find that I have on my hands more than I bargained for. I set out to write a few light sketches of this western coast, and lo, I am amid the foundations of an empire! In my young days I used to read about "the continuous woods"

> "Where rolls the Oregon,
> And hears no sound save its own dashings;"

but now, as I listen, I hear another sound than that of its own dashings—the sound of the wheels of industry; while far off in the valley—and not so very far off either—there swells a muffled roar in the tramp, tramp, of an exceeding great army, coming to take possession.

Historical events are always more striking when they are put in contrast. I can remember when all this northwest coast was set down on the maps as unexplored, a terra incognita, of which the great body of our countrymen knew little and cared less. Indeed, whenever it came up in Congress, it was a favorite subject of ridicule. Senators and Representatives thought it of so little value that it was hardly worth firing a shot to keep it from England, or any other foreign power, that should have the ambition to go in and possess it. The Rocky Mountains were the natural boundary of the

United States, beyond which the country was hardly fit for human habitation—at least for civilized communities—and ought to be left to its natural occupants, the wild Indians and the grizzly bears! In 1844 a bill was before the United States Senate to establish a mail line from Missouri to the Pacific coast, on which Daniel Webster spoke as follows:

> "What do we want with the vast, worthless area, this region of savages and wild beasts, of deserts, of shifting sands and whirlwinds of dust, of cactus and prairie-dogs? To what use could we ever hope to put these great deserts, or these endless mountain ranges, impenetrable, and covered to their base with eternal snow? What can we ever hope to do with the western coast, a coast of three thousand miles, rock-bound, cheerless, and uninviting, and not a harbor on it? What use have we for such a country? Mr. President, I will never vote one cent from the public treasury to place the Pacific Coast one inch nearer to Boston than it is now."

Nor was Mr. Webster alone in this; Mr. Clay and Mr. Calhoun, and other leaders of the Senate, were of the same mind.

But a generation has passed, and a star has risen out of the west—one of the most brilliant on the horizon of our country. The vacant space on the Pacific coast has ceased to be a Territory, and as a State ranks among the largest between the two oceans! Here are a few figures: Pennsylvania covers forty-three thousand square miles; New York, forty-seven thousand; and Washington, seventy thousand! California makes a still larger figure on the map; it has more than twice as many square miles; indeed, it is second in the Union only to Texas. But States are counted rich not by the space they cover, but by their natural products in agriculture or mines. California is made rich by its gold and silver, and Pennsylvania richer still by its enormous beds of coal. Where does the State of Washington come in? Its people tell us that it has more coal than Pennsylvania, more iron than Alabama, and more lumber than Michigan and Wisconsin put together! This would make Washington richer by nature even than California (although, not having been so long settled, it has not half the population), as beds of coal and iron, of which the latter State has little or none, are of far more value than mines of gold and silver. In the productions of a semi-tropical climate—in vineyards and orange groves—California is superior. But in Washington the fruits suited to a more northern latitude are abundant. At the East we count strawberries and other small fruits that have to be cultivated, a luxury. What would our housekeepers say to be offered two dozen baskets for seventy-five cents? In the more important staple of grain, Washington has, on the uplands of the interior, a wheat belt that reminds us of those of Minnesota and Manitoba. It is no uncommon thing for the land to yield from fifty to eighty bushels to the acre. Indeed, in the exhibit of Washington in the World's Fair at Chicago, there were shown one hundred and one bushels of flour as the product of a single acre, while one who rides through the oat-fields may often see stalks nine feet high! The grass is of a sweetness which it retains through all weather. It is not necessary to gather it into barns. It does not spoil when left lying out in the fields, and exposed to the rain, but remains green and juicy, making the most delicious hay for horses. So abundant is it, that cattle can be raised almost for nothing; so that, when offered for sale, a horse will not bring much more than a sheep. A friend told me that he had been offered horses at three dollars apiece, and that he might have his pick out of a hundred for five! Of course, in this case, as he lived in Portland, the price would be quadrupled by the cost of transportation. But the fact shows the abundance and the cheapness of everything on this marvellous Pacific coast.

Such uplands would have a certain majesty even if they were spread out in boundless plains like the steppes of Asia; but how much grander are they when enclosed, like the parks of Colorado, by ranges of mountains! One of these is so begirt with Alpine scenery that it has been reserved, like the Yosemite in California, and the Yellowstone Park in Wyoming, to be for the enjoyment of the people forever. The administration of General Harrison left many good things to the American people, but few of more enduring value than the "Pacific Forest Reserve," which it created in the very heart of the State by withdrawing from entry—that is, from sale and purchase—a tract of land forty-two miles from north to south, and thirty-six miles from east to west; an area one-fifth larger than the State of Rhode Island, and of which it is affirmed that it "contains at once the highest peak, the most extensive glacial system, and the finest natural gardens to be found in the world." Though yet little known to tourists, it will not be long before it is included in the summer trips to the Pacific. Already a wagon road has been built to it, and it is within a day or two's drive from different points on the Northern Pacific Railroad.

But the richest inheritance may be wasted by neglect. The more wonderful it is, the more jealously should it be guarded and kept. The first thing is to protect it from spoliation. The wild wood is the domain of squatters, who range through it at will, and cut down and burn up in a very destructive way. Of course, a certain degree of liberty is to be allowed to the backwoodsmen, who have to camp in the forest with nothing above them but the green leaves. It would be a hard case if a man who has tramped in the woods all day long, and is wet and cold and tired and hungry, could not help himself to wood to kindle a fire to boil his kettle and cook his poor supper. No one would deny him this. But the mischief is that he does not always put out the fire when he moves camp the next morning. It is often left to smoulder, and sometimes blazes up again and spreads till the whole forest is one mighty conflagration. But in time we may hope that the people will appreciate this magnificent park, which is to be not only for them, but for their children after them to the latest generation.

But this Pacific Forest Reserve is in the interior, while we are still on the coast, which we must not leave without emphasizing the point that all the resources and all the riches of the State of Washington are doubled and quadrupled by the mere fact of its position. If it could change places with Montana, it would not be worth a quarter of what it is now, for the simple reason that the value of its products depends not merely on the fact that they are good for food, but that they can be got to market—to the places where they are wanted for the support of human beings. If the uplands of Montana could be made to wave with the golden grain, it would be a question whether it would pay to raise it and ship it, as, by the time it got into the hands of the consumer, he would have to pay not only for the raising, but for the transporting, so that his "penny loaf" would come pretty dear when it came to be put into the hungry mouths of a family of lusty boys, with excellent appetites!

But the farmers of Washington have no trouble in getting rid of their crops, for behold the carriers of the sea are already at the door! The people of Seattle and Tacoma look down upon the great hulls lying at their wharves, which they can fill in a few hours by simply opening their elevators, when these great birds of the ocean will spread their wings and fly away to China or to any point of Eastern Asia!

I have been studying the chart of the Pacific, which the Secretary of the Chamber of Commerce at Tacoma gave me, and find it full of interest and full of suggestion as to the lines which the commerce of the Pacific will take. Look northward at our coast-line, how the continent throws out its arms to the west till it almost touches the shores of Asia. What a graceful curve is that of the Aleutian Islands towards the Siberian coast! These islands are so many stepping-stones, a sort of Giant's Causeway, for the advance of America towards Asia.

To be sure, the first sight of Asia is not very inviting, for over against the last island rises the rugged and storm-beaten coast of Kamschatka, which carries terror in its very name, as it seems to speak of icebergs and the pitiless cold and the long darkness of the Arctic night.

But, after all, Nature is a gentle mother, and if now and then she affrights us, again she quiets our fears by providing a refuge against our dangers. And so in this very case, only a few weeks since, a captain in our navy told me the finest port in which he had ever dropped anchor in any part of the world—not excepting the Bay of Rio Janeiro or the Bay of Naples—was that of Petropaulovski in Kamschatka.*

Looking on the map again, I find the name of another Russian port on the Pacific, Vladivostock, to which it is directing the great transcontinental railroad which it has long been pushing across Siberia, a movement to which increased importance has been given by the recent war between Japan and China—a war that has changed the relations towards each other of those two great powers of Eastern Asia, but has not changed our relations to either, for we are the friends of both. In the midst of wars and rumors of wars, it is the proud position of our country to stand apart among the mighty combatants as the one that has no traditional hatreds, no grudges to satisfy, no wrongs to avenge, no longings for more territory, no desire to be a great military power; its only ambition to be the mediator and peacemaker among nations, the friend of the whole human race!

---

* The officer here referred to is Captain Berry, whom many will recall as in command of the Michigan, which lay off Chicago during the Exposition. He is a Kentuckian, of splendid physique, with a frame of iron, who can be relied upon to do whatever man can do in any perilous enterprise, and who for that reason was ordered to the Arctic Ocean some years ago to search for the Jeannette, which had been sent out on an exploring expedition, under Captain De Long, and had not returned. He found that it had been crushed in the ice, and that its brave captain, and the greater part of his crew, had perished with cold and hunger. To complete the tale of catastrophes, Berry's own ship was destroyed by fire off the coast of Asia, and he was obliged to make his way on sledges across the whole of Siberia, without even a tent to cover him; sleeping on the snow, with nothing above him but the stars, when the thermometer was fifty degrees below zero!

CHAPTER XVIII

THE CITY OF PORTLAND

In leaving Tacoma we leave the sea, and turn southward, as if we were bound for California. The day's ride is through a country that is for the most part a wilderness, though here and there the woodman's axe has made a little clearing, and let the sunlight into the gloom of the forest; and a few poor dwellings furnish shelter for the lumbermen or fishermen. The one event of the day, the only break in the boundless monotony, is the crossing of the Columbia River. No bridge spans it, for it is so broad, and at times so tremendous in its flood, that a bridge could be built only at an enormous cost; but the train is run upon a ferryboat of huge proportions, on which it is floated across the broad current. Once on the other side, our course is along its banks, or in sight of it, so that from our window we are close to an ocean steamer coming in from the sea. Thus railway and river run parallel till both reach the chief city of Oregon.

As soon as we were in the streets of Portland, I felt at home. An Eastern man can hardly come here without being struck with the resemblance to the cities of New England; while, as to the people, he is apt to say in his homely phrase, "They are our folks!" Oregon was settled before California, and drew to it a different kind of population. The rush to the latter began with the discovery of gold in 1848, but long before that, the report of the famous Willamette Valley, which was said to be rich as the Valley of the Nile, drew to it the eyes of Eastern farmers, many of whom crossed the plains with their ox teams to find homes in this agricultural paradise. Such sturdy pioneers gave a character to the new settlements on the Pacific coast.*

---

* Mr. George H. Himes, whose father was among the early settlers of Oregon and who is himself an authority in all matters as to its history, gives me the following details :

"Gold was first discovered in California January 19, 1848, by James W. Marshall, an Oregon pioneer of 1844. He went to California in 1845, and hired out to Captain John A. Sutter, who came to Oregon in 1838, and went to Colorado in the latter part of 1839. It was in 1849 that the great rush to the gold fields occurred, it having taken a year for the discovery to become known east of the Mississippi. While the Methodist missionaries, Daniel and Jason Lee, came in 1834, followed by the A. B. C. F. M. missionaries, Dr. Samuel Parker, Dr. Whitman, Rev. H. H. Spalding, Rev. Elkanah Walker, and Rev. Cushing Eells, who came in 1835-38, it was not until 1842 that any regular immigrants—home builders, in the best sense—came to Oregon. The letters of the foregoing missionaries doubtless had much to do with this initial immigration. Then in 1843 Dr. Whitman, who left here in October, 1842, returned with a large immigration—one thousand souls. This fixed Oregon for the United States, and practically settled the Oregon question, which had been in controversy for twenty-five years; although the formal and official settlement of it was not announced until June 15, 1846. The meeting of the General Assembly of the Presbyterian Church was held here just half a century after the first home builders came.

"Speaking of Dr. Parker reminds me that it was his lectures through Northeastern Pennsylvania in 1839-42, after his return from Oregon via the Sandwich Islands, which first gave my father the impulse to come to Oregon. He started in 1847, when I was

After the war there was a migration, not large, but of picked men, who had been in the army. An old soldier told me that he came here right after Appomattox, and that he walked all the way across the plains. It took him four months; but he said that he never enjoyed anything more in his life. And well he might. It was an easier transition for him to ordinary life, than if he had gone back to the old shop or the old farm, for here at least he could keep up a little of the military habit, as he was ever on the march, dwelling in tents, or sleeping on the ground and looking up to the stars! There was an exhilaration in this free life, as there was in the very air of the plains; and as he strode along he seemed to hear the tramp, tramp, of the long column behind him; and if he did not hear the blast of the bugle, he could at least lift up his voice, singing "The Red, White, and Blue" or "The Battle Cry of Freedom." By this endurance of hardship he proved his manhood and his right to the noblest title that his country could give, that of an American citizen. This is the stuff to make a State of, and such were the founders of the noble commonwealth of Oregon.

As was the State so was the city, which did not spring up, like Jonah's gourd, in a night, but grew slowly and solidly, as a city builded, not by adventurers in search of

---

three years old, but only came as far as Illinois. The journey was resumed in 1853, and after seven months' constant travelling, we reached Puget Sound, then in Oregon. Ours was the first through immigrant train—thirty-six wagons, and about one hundred persons—that entered direct what is now the State of Washington. We came through the Cascade Mountains a few miles south of where the Northern Pacific Railroad now crosses, making our own road as we journeyed."

gold, but by men of substance and of character. Hence Portland has not at all the roughness of many Western towns, where the streets are half paved and the houses half built. On the contrary, it has a finished and substantial appearance that would become any Eastern city. As I went about the streets, I was constantly reminded of the beautiful cities of New England, and kept saying to myself: "This is Hartford! This is Springfield! This is Worcester!"

Nor is it merely in the outward appearance, for Portland has all the elements of substantial prosperity. In the vast trade of the northwest, San Francisco has the lead in the seal fishery, even though John Jacob Astor began his operations in 1811 at the mouth of the Columbia, where the little port of Astoria preserves the name of the thrifty German who was the founder of the fur trade on our western coast. But in the salmon fishery, which has sprung up in our day, Portland, as it is some hundreds of miles nearer the place of the enormous "catch," has more of the business of supplying the markets of the world; as it leads also in the lumber that is sent landward and seaward, not only to the towns and cities of the interior, but to the Sandwich Islands and to Japan and China.

With such elements of wealth, it is not surprising that Portland has grown rich, till its banking houses rank among the soundest on all the exchanges of the country. We who have been accustomed to talk of the solid men of Boston may speak of the solid men of Portland.

But Portland is more than a rich city; it is a city of schools and churches. As the Israelites carried the ark in all their wanderings, the sons of the Pilgrims carry the meeting-house and the school-house, which are the first objects to catch the eye in any city, town, or village, whithersoever they come. In Portland the public schools are among the most conspicuous buildings of the city, while churches lift their spires on all sides.

As I hear the people talk about the men whom they hold most in reverence and in honor, I cannot but think that the city owes much to the peculiar character of its founders, and especially to a few of a strong personality which impressed itself upon the character of the rising city. Two names I hear most often mentioned—that of Judge Deady, the ornament of the bar and the bench, whose recent death is greatly mourned; and that of Rev. Dr. Lindsley, who, as the pastor of the First Presbyterian Church for many years, was, by his position as well as his ability, the leader of his brethren. The names of such men should be held forever in grateful remembrance. Dr. Lindsley was a sort of Presbyterian bishop, who had the care of all the churches. The "Old First" of Portland has been a mother of churches, giving freely to scores if not to hundreds of missionary churches on the Pacific coast. It was a fit recognition of its importance that brought the General Assembly of the Presbyterian Church all the way across the continent to hold its meeting with a church that bore an historic name.

This church had a pastor worthy of its past reputation in Rev. Dr. Arthur J. Brown, a son of New England, but who, by one sacred association, belongs to the whole country. One of the earliest recollections of his childhood was that of seeing his father leave the old home to take his place in the ranks of those who were fighting for their country. He enlisted for three years, on the very last day of which, as he was about to return to his home, he fell, and only his silent form was brought back to be laid in a soldier's grave. To one with such heroic blood in his veins, we look to see him bearing a manly part in any sphere of duty to which he may be called, and we are not disappointed. Even the highest place on the Pacific coast has been thought by his brethren not to be the full measure of his ability and usefulness to the Church at large; and since we left that coast he has been called to New York to take the place of the lamented Arthur Mitchell, as Secretary of the Board of Foreign Missions.

As I came to Portland in midsummer, I found Dr. Brown divided in his thoughts between the care of his church, and plans for his vacation, which was near at hand. No one is better entitled to a respite than the hard-worked pastor of a city church with a thousand members. He was going off with his brother Morrison, the excellent pastor of Calvary Church, and their families, to camp near the foot of Mount Hood, sixty miles east, where they could pitch their tents under the trees, and spend some weeks in hunting and fishing. With his cordial hospitality he invited me to go along; but I declined with thanks, for I do not take my vacations in that way. If I had lived in the days of the apostles, they would not have had me in their boat, for I don't fish; Peter would have thrown me overboard as unfit for the profession. Nor am I a mighty hunter before the Lord; for, to tell the truth, I hate the crack of a rifle! I shall be content to hear of the prowess of those who go forth to battle in the achievements of the Presbyterian Nimrods on the slopes of Mount Hood.

But if we did not go a-fishing, we did make the excursion up the Columbia, the scenery of which has hardly its equal in the Old World or the New. Great rivers, like great men, have to get their reputation by fighting for it. Almost all the great rivers of Europe have their sources in the Alps, from which they come down by leaps and waterfalls, till they are confronted by huge cliffs crossing their path, through which they have to cut their way. Thus are formed the innumerable gorges through which the Rhine and the Danube make their long journeys from the mountains to the sea. The same forces have been at work on the Columbia with the same result, reminding us at once of the Iron Gates of the Danube, and of the cliffs below the Falls at Niagara, where the rocky heights, cleft in twain, look down on the rapids and whirlpools in which the mad current rushes on its way. It needs no geologist to trace the path of the destroyer, for we can see it for ourselves. So near did we pass to the cliffs on the Columbia, that, as we sat on deck, they seemed to hang right over us; and as the scenery grew wilder and wilder, the captain took us into the pilot house that we might keep an eye on both sides at once. In rounding "Cape Horn," we passed within a few feet of giant columns that seemed as if they might bear up the very gates of heaven on their mighty shoulders.

But let no one think that the scenery of the Columbia is all majesty and terror. True, the mountains are dark, but the waters that spring out of them, as they pour down the mountain side, shine and glisten in a way to give relief to the most forbidding background. Look up at the "Bridal Veil"! Was ever a waterfall more fitly named? The sheet of spray that leaps in air seems, indeed, like a delicate drapery of lace flung over the form of the mountain beauty that hides behind.

On our return, an old resident of Portland, Mr. George

H. Himes, called to offer his services to take me to some points of observation outside the city that most visitors do not see. He frankly confessed that he was a crank in these matters, and that took my heart at once, for I am fond of cranks, at least when the mania takes the mild form of a passionate love of nature. He wanted to take me to a hill a few miles out of town to see the sun rise, when we should have the whole panorama spread out before us.

"But at what hour must we set out?"

He hesitated a little, and then said softly: "The earlier the better!"

"And what do you call early?"

"What would you say to starting at half-past four?"

"All right; I shall expect you at that hour."

Of course, we both expressed our desire to have Dr. Brown join us, but when he heard the hour, he respectfully declined. We did not press him, for he is an elderly gentleman, thirty-seven years old, and could not be expected to break the blissful calm of "tired nature's sweet restorer" at that unconscionable hour. But as I am a boy of seventy-two, I am under no law of time or place. The very thought of the coming pleasure caused me to wake in the night, eager with anticipation, until, unable to wait any longer, I rose and dressed, and, looking at my watch, found that it was just four! Better too soon than too late, and I muffled myself up in a thick overcoat, and took my seat on the veranda of the Portland Hotel. At half-past four exactly a light buggy drove in, and we stole out of the yard as if we were engaged in some criminal enterprise. As the plank roads and asphalt pavements give but little sound, we crept softly out of the city, and began to wind our way up the hills.

As soon as we were in the woods, my friend's enthusiasm for trees came out, for he is a lover, I might almost say a worshipper, of trees, and knows the trunk and branches, the bark and leaf, of every tree on the mountains, and with natural pride he pointed out to me the Oregon cedar, that is invaluable for building purposes, as it will stand the storms of a hundred years; and the Douglas fir, or, more accurately, the Douglas spruce, of which there are specimens in a park near the city two hundred and fifty feet high!

As we climbed higher and higher, the landscape below us spread out wider and wider, till it was like the plain of Damascus as I looked back upon it from the side of Anti-Lebanon. To be sure, Damascus is not here, but in what nature has done for both, I could say truly that the Columbia is far greater and more majestic than "Abana and Pharpar, rivers of Damascus"—and I might add, "than all the waters of Israel"—as it rolls its mighty volume to the sea.

But that was not all that we had come to see. The great sight from this point of view is the mountains on the horizon—Mount Rainier (or Tacoma), Mount Adams, Mount Hood, Mount Saint Helen's, and Mount Jefferson —all with their crowns of snow that shine gloriously when touched by the morning sun. But in this we were disappointed. The mountains were all there, and we were there to see them; but the sun did not show his face. My friend was full of apologies for his bad behavior. But, as I am an old traveller, I am used to disappointments. Had I not, when in Japan, made a journey of seventy miles to get a near view of Fusiyama, and then he wrapped himself in clouds, as if disdaining the homage of a foreigner! These rebuffs of nature I take with philosophy; and to-day, **if we had not seen** all, **we had seen** enough to repay our climb. It was enough to see the awakening of the world to life; to hear the **song of** birds; and to see the gradual lifting of the clouds from the tops of the mountains, which were beginning to be touched with golden light, as if nature were offering her morning sacrifice.

At half-past seven we rode into the courtyard of **the hotel, not only** content with **our** three hours' ride of **the morning, but so** well satisfied that **we** were ready **to** repeat it that very evening, and at eight o'clock set out once more for the hills. The scene by night was, in some respects, more glorious than by day; for, as the city is lighted by electricity, it seemed as if the thousands of stars above were reflected in the plain below—an illumination that extended beyond the river to the lights of Vancouver, the military post for the Department of the Columbia, ten miles away. It required but little imagination to see in these the camp-fires of some mighty Asiatic host (like that of Sennacherib when he came up against Jerusalem) that had pitched their tents in the valley.

The next day we said good-by to Portland, **where in less** than a week we had come to feel at home. **So** quickly are minds and hearts fused by sympathy, that those who are strangers one day are acquaintances the next, and then friends. No one can **help** feeling respect for a people who, by their own unaided strength, have made a foremost position in our great Confederacy of **States.** We are proud of them as our kindred, of the same New England stock, whose intelligence and force of will and power of achievement reflect honor, not only upon themselves, but upon the whole American Union to which they and we belong.

CHAPTER XIX

HOMEWARD BOUND—THE STRIKES

WHEN the hour of departure had come our friends, who were at the station to see us off, congratulated us that we could now go in safety. The strikes of the summer were nowhere more violent than on the Pacific coast, and the railroads were tied up so that it was impossible to move. A gentleman and his wife from New York, who came on with us, had been shut up in Portland for a month. Another passenger, who was from California, told me that it had taken him twenty-two days to get to Portland! He had started from Sacramento and got into the mountains, but from that point could not stir a step. As soon as a train was made up, the strikers would uncouple the passenger cars from the engine. This paralysis of communication might have continued for months, had not the Government put forth its strong hand. But as soon as the bluecoats were distributed along the lines, the strikers began to see things in a new light. At Tacoma I had met Colonel Anderson, the second in command of the Department at Vancouver, who told me that he thought the coast was clear; but for all that, I was not at all displeased to see a stalwart soldier in the cab with the engineer, and others on the train, and others still at every station on the road.

The terminus of the Northern Pacific Road is not at

Portland, but at Tacoma, to which we had to return to take a fair start. Here we changed our course from north to east, and as we moved out, towards midnight, felt that at last we were indeed homeward bound. Had I known then as much as I know now, I would not have stolen away by night, but waited till broad daylight, to see more of the grand scenery of the Pacific coast; for, during these hours of darkness, we were to cross the Cascade Range, where the road plays hide-and-seek, now rushing into dark tunnels, and then reappearing at some unexpected point, never taking a straight course, but always winding round and round, once, I believe, executing a spiral in the very heart of the mountain—a feat of engineering that excited my amazement when I saw it in crossing the Alps from Italy to Switzerland, by the Pass of the St. Gothard. Where this sudden whirl is not necessary, it makes a circuit on the mountain side, always with an up grade, till it attains an elevation of four or five thousand feet. Certainly this is all that is required for its dignity as it launches out on its voyage across the continent.

And now, before I start on this "voyage," I feel it to be a duty to recognize the immense service rendered by this great national highway, not only to the western coast, but to our whole country. It is so long since we had the first of these transcontinental roads, that to recall the state we were in before that time reads like ancient history. But there are a good many of us who are old enough to remember it well; and still more, when not only was there no such road in existence, but when many who had been over the ground, and knew the tremendous obstacles in the way, said that the very idea of it was chimerical! It was well enough to talk about, but to construct a railway across a whole continent—from ocean to ocean—was simply impossible. Probably they would have been of the same opinion still, but that, while they were reasoning against it, the thing was done! It was no longer necessary to take an ocean voyage, and cross the Isthmus of Panama, and then take another voyage, to reach California; since one could step into a car in New York and step out of it in Oakland, across the bay from San Francisco!

But this was only the beginning of good things. To most of those who had looked on in amazement it seemed that the first must be the last. So reasoned men of great sagacity. Soon after the war there was a council of military men on our western border to fix the location of forts to protect the frontier against the Indians. Among them was General Sherman, who had lived in California, and felt the importance of a close connection between the eastern and western coast. And yet he and the other officers and engineers thought it would require a long course of years to carry out a work of such magnitude, and all agreed that one road would be ample for the needs of the country for a quarter of a century! "Yet," said General Sherman, when telling the story, "in three years from that time I was riding over the road to San Francisco"—to which we may add that at the end of the quarter of a century there are, including the Canadian Pacific, no less than six through lines from the Atlantic to the Pacific.

These roads have revolutionized the country. They have brought the distant near, so that the mid-continent and the Pacific coast are within touch of the rich and populous East. As they opened new territories, armies of emigrants have marched in to take possession, and the yield of the prairies has doubled the produce of American harvests, which, with the opening of mines of gold and silver, has added literally thousands of millions to the national wealth. Seeing all this, I confess that I am indignant at the attacks so often made upon the projectors and builders of these great lines of railroads. As to their motives, they may be like other men; but as to the results of what they have done, they are among the greatest benefactors to their country and to mankind.

The morning after we had crossed the Cascade Mountains, we opened our eyes on a scene that was neither beautiful nor sublime, as we saw before us only a plain of vast extent, unrelieved by mountain or forest—a land that seemed to be smitten with a curse, upon which nothing grew but sage brush, or other coarse grasses, which only a camel, used to crop the short and bitter herbage of the desert, would touch! And yet, as I looked out upon this boundless desolation, something within me whispered, "Why dost thou curse what God hath not cursed? Knowest thou not that this very plain is only a part of what was called on the old maps 'The Great American Desert'? Yet the pioneers of California soon found that it needed only the gentle showers from heaven, or the springs that run among the hills, to become like the garden of the Lord!"

So this soil has all the elements of vegetation, and needs only the water from above or from below, from the springs or the skies, to burst forth into life and beauty. This we saw, as we were soon in the heart of the wheat belt of the State of Washington. Where not sown with wheat, the land is given up to grass. Thousands of acres were covered with the new-mown hay. And such hay! "Sir," said an enthusiastic inhabitant of the country, pointing out of the window, "it is the finest hay in the world! Look at it! It is not like your Eastern hay, that dries up till it has no more juice in it than chips!" I saw that the hay that was lying in the fields, exposed to sun and rain, was as fresh and green as if it had been newly mown. He would have me put it to another test. "Try it!" he said; "put it in your mouth and taste it, and see how sweet and juicy it is!" I did not deem it necessary to make the experiment, but could believe all that he said of it, and of the general fertility of the country, for which nature has done everything— if it is not destroyed by the folly of man!

I make this qualification, as we were now in the centre of strikes. We saw no outbreak, but around all the stations were groups of men, who were in an angry mood. They attempted no violence, but stood, or sat on the fences, a little way off, sullen and defiant. What they *would* have done must be left to conjecture, had they not been restrained by another figure that appeared on the scene in the person of the army officer who walked up and down the platform with an air of quiet determination that meant business. I could not resist the impulse to go up to him and give him a hearty shake of the hand, thanking God in my heart that he had come to the front for such a time as this. Nor was I less interested in the soldiers, brave and manly fellows, who had no swagger about them, but who were under strict discipline, and knew their duty and were ready to do it.

Among the regiments that had been ordered to this service was one of colored troops, who were not a whit behind their white fellow-soldiers in martial spirit. Every man had his loins girded up with his belt filled with cartridges as if the fate of the country depended on him.

I could but be amused at the air of possession—surely possession is nine points of the law—with which these stalwart black fellows marched up and down the platform, while the strikers kept at a respectful distance. Good for you, my brave fellows! I said in my heart. As long as you keep guard on this station those idlers will keep quiet, till by and by they may get tired of sitting on the fence, and get down and go to work again.

The meeting with the soldiers was always a pleasant episode, but the necessity for such a guard all along the line was a serious matter, for the dangers were real and great. The streams in this country have worn deep gorges, which are spanned by bridges of great length, thereby offering opportunity, not only for wreck and ruin of property, but for a fearful destruction of life. But a few days before, the strikers at Sacramento had undermined a bridge, so that a car was wrecked, killing a party of soldiers. Several times to-day we were exposed to the same fate. Once, as we were creeping over a trestle at a snail's pace, I put my head out of the window, and looking down saw that we were more than a hundred feet in air, so that if the bridge had given way, not a passenger would have been left to tell the tale. I should have held my breath in apprehension had I not at the same moment seen, in the valley below, the white tents that showed that the soldiers were keeping guard over our safety. The same precautions were taken at every tunnel, where an explosion of dynamite in the middle might have left us blocked in the heart of a mountain. But here again the boys in blue saluted us as we rushed into the darkness, and again as we came out with flying colors. God bless their brave and manly hearts!

It was a long day's ride across the State of Washington, for this is a country of magnificent distances; and it was late in the afternoon when we reached Spokane Falls, a town that ranks next to Seattle and Tacoma in the State. The very name indicates the source of its prosperity, as its falls, which include a succession of rapids, furnish a water power hardly equalled in the United States, except at Niagara—a power sufficient to set thousands of wheels in motion, and to supply the demands of a hundred different industries. Just now the wheels are *not* in motion; the mills are shut down, and the men that were employed in them stand round the streets, with their hands in their pockets, accusing their late employers of being responsible for their present idleness.

Dr. Mundy, the pastor of the Presbyterian Church, who met me at the station, gave me a pitiful account of the general prostration in the business of the country. Never was there such a paralysis of industry. Nor is it only in Spokane, but north of this is a region, which bears the poetical name of Cœur d'Alene, that is equally distinguished for the beauty of its lakes, and its mines of gold and silver. Yet even here the evil spirit has entered, and the mining population has assumed such fierce mastery that the quiet, peaceable inhabitants are living in a state of terror. This industrial stagnation is always a danger to the public peace. Idle men are dangerous men. Satan finds mischief for idle hands. Men who are out of employment do not accuse themselves for what they suffer; while they brood over their troubles, they never ascribe them to their own want of foresight, or economy, in providing for a rainy day, but charge them wholly to the selfishness of the rich, which makes them eager for riot and revolution.

Of course, one cannot but sympathize with men who are willing to work, and find nothing to do. To preach patience is easy for those who do not have to exercise it. The only consolation is that the depression here is but a part of that which has spread all over the country, and must pass away with the general return of better times. There are few cities for which nature has done so much as for Spokane Falls, whose position is like that of Lawrence and Lowell in Massachusetts; and here, as there, the wheels of industry must soon begin to move.

Even had our thoughts been somewhat gloomy, they must have been dispelled as we left Spokane, and kept for miles along the banks of the river which bears that name, whose swift current is a fit emblem of the perpetual life and activity of the American people.

When I left Dr. Mundy standing on the platform at Spokane, I felt that I had left my last acquaintance behind. But I was soon to make another. As we took our places again in the drawing-room car and looked round at the new-comers, I saw an old man, who had somewhat of a military bearing, as, indeed, the button on his coat indicated that he had been a soldier of our war. As he was sitting alone, with no companion but a little dog, I gave him the greeting of a stranger, which led to a conversation that was to me one of great interest. Though he was not seventy years old, he had served in different armies and in different parts of the world.

As to his family, he told me that he was born in Ireland, in Turlough, in the County Mayo, and was the youngest of eighteen brothers, and the twenty-first of twenty-two children! His father was a commissioned officer in the English army in the Forty-seventh Regiment, and fought under Wellington at Waterloo. Perchance the martial fire of the old man communicated itself to this son, who, when but eighteen years of age, enlisted as a private soldier in the Fortieth Regiment (Second Somersetshire), and sailed for India. Landing at Calcutta, he went up the Ganges and finally crossed the Himalayas, and found himself at Cabul, the capital of Afghanistan. He was in the Sikh War, under General Sale, who was killed at Cabul, after which General Nott took command, under whom he marched to Candahar and to Guznee. That he was a good soldier was shown by the following: One day as his regiment was drawn up on parade, he heard a voice calling his name, with a command to come to the front! It made him tremble, for he looked for nothing but a reprimand, but stepped forward, when the commanding officer dismounted from his horse, and, taking him by the hand, declared him a commissioned officer in the service of Her Majesty the Queen! That was the proudest day of his life.

After five years of service in India, he returned to England, and in 1852 came to America, landing in New York, where he had letters to Dr. Tyng and Dr. Muhlenberg. For a time he was a colporteur of the Tract Society; after which he went to Pelham Priory, and was with Rev. Cornelius Wilton Bolton. Thus his associations seemed to have been always among the good—good soldiers and good men.

In 1855 he went to Kansas, where a sympathy of ideas led him to become an associate of John Brown in his revolutionary schemes, and he would have been with him at Harper's Ferry had he not been detailed to conduct some fugitive slaves from Detroit into Canada. When the war came on he hesitated to enter the army from conscientious scruples. He was willing to take an oath to support the Constitution, but not the Fugitive Slave Law! The recruiting officer thought that that disqualified him, and between them he remained in suspense for six weeks; but Governor Thomas Kearney made a quick end of the business, saying, " He'll do ; muster him in!" So he entered in 1861, was captain of a company, and fought at Wilson's Creek in Missouri, where General Lyon was killed ; at Osceola ; at Pea Ridge ; and marched south to join in the movement of General Banks up the Red River; after which he was kept on duty in Missouri and Arkansas, and the Cherokee country.

During the war the old man told me that he was never under fire that he did not think of his mother, and mentally resolved, if spared, to go and see her; but it was not till 1867 that he was able to carry out his wish. Then he sailed for the old country, and landing in Ireland, made his way to the village which he had left so many years before, and followed the familiar path which led to the thatched cottage which he recognized as the old home! Knocking at the door, he asked if he could find a lodging, but the maid said he must go on to the village, where he would find the inn. But gently forcing his way in, he saw an old lady in her chair, who asked where he came from? to which he answered, "From America." "Ah, America!" she said, as if the very word awakened sad memories; "I once had a son there, but now I don't know where he is." This was too much for her wandering boy, who said, "Mother, don't you know me?" The old man wiped his eyes as he spoke of his mother, who was in her ninetieth year; while to her it was as if her son had been dead and was alive again.

After this pious duty was performed, he returned to

America and went to California, from which he came North, and for the last eleven years has been at, or near, Spokane, in the service of the Northern Pacific Railroad Company. Now that his working days are over, he is going East to visit his children and grandchildren in Brooklyn, after which he will settle at Toronto, to pass the rest of his days.

All this was told with the utmost simplicity, with no boasting of what he had been or had done; but that only made it the more touching, as it showed that the truest manhood does not belong only to those who are at the top, but quite as often to those who serve in the ranks, and whose courage and devotion are too often undiscovered because they are hidden under the surface of common life.

CHAPTER XX

MONTANA—THE VIGILANTES

IN leaving Spokane Falls we do not leave the Spokane River, any more than in leaving Niagara Falls we leave the Niagara River. In both cases the rush of the Falls communicates itself to the waters below, which whirl and foam and then rush onward, as if in pursuit of a beholder who should flee from the sight in terror. So when we left Spokane, the river seemed to be chasing us, and we were running a race along its banks. But after a few miles we had to part company, leaving it to continue its course till it empties into the Columbia; while we turned in another direction to find a passage through the mountains. A glance at the map is sufficient to show the enormous engineering difficulties in the construction of the Northern Pacific. But the rugged defiles are picturesque as the passes of the Alps, while in lakes it would be difficult to find in Switzerland anything more exquisitely beautiful than the Pend d'Oreille. Here we are in the State of Idaho (how musical are these Indian names!), but of which we see little, as we pass through what may be called its Pan Handle, its boundary being not by degrees of latitude or longitude, but by the trend of a chain of mountains which runs from northwest to southeast, and we are at the small end; while farther south it broadens to proportions that place it alongside its great sister States.

Before I left New York for the Pacific coast, a missionary in Idaho kindly invited me to visit him in his Western home, presenting a picture of the scenery round him that was most tempting. That I could not bring it into my tour was my loss; and I can only assure him that my passion for travelling has only been stimulated by the experience of the last summer, and that when I am a few years *younger* (as I seem to be growing that way), it is not impossible that I may visit Idaho, and describe, with youthful enthusiasm, its lakes and rivers, its mountains and valleys. But for the present my friend will excuse me if I leave, without further observation, a State that we passed through chiefly in the night.

But the next morning, when the sun rose gloriously over the mountains of Montana, we could not restrain our enthusiasm. Here we had no excuse for silence, for we crossed the State in broad daylight; and, as it was a long midsummer day, we could sit at our windows from daybreak till evening twilight, taking in the ever-changing views all round the horizon. That day I took to Montana, as if I had been an old settler. Its very name is attractive, as it is significant of the character of the country, whose chief feature is its mountains, in which it resembles the north of Scotland, the mere suggestion of which is enough to stir the blood of one whose "heart's in the Highlands."

Wherever such romantic tastes still exist, they can find abundant gratification in almost any part of the great mountain chain that includes Colorado, and north of which is Montana. We have not, indeed, in our Western Hemisphere any "Roof of the World" like that in Asia in the Himalayas. But our continent has its rise and fall, like the billows of the sea, and there is a gradual ascent from the valley of the Mississippi, over a thousand miles of plain, to the great plateau that culminates in the Rocky Mountains and their extensions north and south, which may be considered as the backbone of the continent.

In speaking thus admiringly of these Western mountains, I do not mean to hold them up as being so high or so difficult of ascent as to test the muscle or the nerve of Alpine climbers. I have no idea of tempting Dr. Parkhurst to leave Switzerland for Montana, for he would be disappointed, since he would find no such awful heights as those of Mont Blanc and the Matterhorn. If, indeed, he wishes to try his cool head and firm step on some mountain this side the sea, let him go to Alaska, and a day or two farther north than we went, he will find himself at the foot of Mount Saint Elias, a monarch of the upper air, to which I am sure that he will, with his usual politeness, take off his hat with profound respect. And then let him put himself in training, and when he is in prime condition make the attempt. He may succeed where others have failed.

But if Montana has no Saint Elias nor Matterhorn, she has mountains enough to fill all her horizons, so that one can hardly go anywhere without having some snow-capped peak in sight.

And the beauty of our western State, as set over against Switzerland, is that our mountains look down upon scenes of plenty, such as Mont Blanc and the Matterhorn never saw. Between the long ranges of Montana are valleys of unbounded fertility. One familiar with the country told me that he had never seen such wheat fields as those near Mussola, a hundred and twenty-five miles west of Helena. One of the great land-owners told him that he had in a single field a thousand acres of oats that stood nine feet high, into which a man could not venture without being lost, as in the depths of an African forest! Fields that are less suited for cultivation are admirably adapted for grazing. One of the sights of every year is the countless herds, bred in Texas, that are driven north to get " hardened " in the bracing air of the uplands of Montana. One riding over the country may literally see the cattle on a thousand hills. "The valleys also are covered over with corn; they shout for joy; they also sing."

It was about noon when we drew up at Helena, not in the town, but in sight of it, for it does not lie on the open plain, but reaches back up into the hills (into a gulch rich in golden ore, which was indeed the attraction that drew the first settlers to this spot), from which the capital looks down on the broad expanse at its feet. As the train made but a brief stop, we saw only just enough to excite our curiosity without gratifying it; so that we were but too glad when, ten days later, after our visit to the Yellowstone Park, we had an opportunity to return and spend a couple of days in Helena, with a visit to Butte and Anaconda, two of the great mining centres of the country.

Meanwhile, **our first glimpse was enough to set us on the track of inquiry, and we were so fortunate as to be thrown with those who were able to answer our questions—the Attorney-General of the State and an editor,** whom I felt at liberty to address as one of the fraternity. Montana has been a rich subject for journalists, not so much because of its mines, as because of its tragic history in the days when the Vigilantes fought with robbers and murderers in a life-and-death struggle between savagery and civilization. I am afraid I did not begin my inquiries in the most flattering way. It could hardly exalt their State pride to hear a stranger say: "I am told that Butte (the great mining centre) is the wickedest town in the world!" to which the Attorney-General, as the official defender of the State, at once made answer: "Butte is no worse than New York! The only difference is that certain forms of wickedness, which you repress by law, are here legalized, so that what in your city is done in secret is here done openly." He made a point of this, as if it were to the credit of Butte, that it had no false shame; and made no attempt to hide its black spots behind bolted doors. "In Butte," he said, "it is no more of a crime to keep a gambling house than to keep a hotel. As the passion for gambling is one that cannot be repressed among miners, we think it is in the interest of morality to have it public rather than private, and so we license it, as you in New York license drinking saloons. And not only so, but here the law requires that the character of the place shall be declared in the sign LEGALIZED GAMBLING, which shall be painted over the door in letters four inches long!"

This was indeed taking the bull by the horns. That his statement was true, I saw a week or two later, when a friend showed me about the streets of Butte. We found, as he had said, that the gambling houses were public institutions; that they were not hidden away in back streets, but stood on the Broadway of the town, with doors wide open to all comers. As my friend led the way I walked in, as I had into the gambling house at Monte Carlo, and here, as there, saw the games in full blast. It must be confessed that there is one advantage in this; that a man cannot hide his wickedness; if he is a gambler, everybody will know it. Young clerks cannot sneak into these places, and spend the money of their employers. So far, its publicity is a protection to those who might suffer from an immorality that was concealed. But on the other hand, there is a terrible temptation in these doors that stand wide open on the street, where every passer-by can hear the rattle of the dice, mingled with the sound of music and dancing. Monte Carlo, as everybody knows who has been in the south of France, is one of the most fascinating places of amusement in Europe; but the more splendid it is, the wider is the gate to destruction, and the more will there be that go in thereat.

This talk about the present state of manners and morals set me a-thinking of the early days of Montana, of which I had read a good deal years ago, and it all came back now that I was on the spot, and could talk with the very men who had taken part in those terrible scenes. The first population that came into this country was attracted by the discovery of gold, a magnet that drew together the good and the bad. The most of the newcomers were honest and hard-working men. But the wealth they dug from the mine was of less value because of the difficulty of shipping it to the East. There were no railroads in those days, and every package of bullion had to be sent overland in mail coaches, across long stretches of country, over mountains and rivers and plains, through dark forests, where there was every opportunity for attack and capture. The chance of booty was so great that it drew together hundreds of desperate criminals who had found the older States too hot to hold them. They formed themselves into bands, and, hiding in some dark glen, waited till their accomplices near the mines sent word that a large shipment would be made on a certain day; when, as the coach climbed slowly up a hill, or was in some deep gorge, there sprang up a dozen men with masked faces and levelled guns, who commanded a halt, and (while the passengers stood trembling) divided the spoil. If there was any resistance, they added murder to robbery. In this way many disappeared whose bones were afterwards found in some lonely place in the forest.

Such was the state of things that had been going on for months, till, through this whole mining country, there was a reign of terror. The discovery that some men who had been supposed to be honest were implicated in these robberies, created such a feeling of suspicion that a man hardly dared to trust his neighbor, till at last the very enormity of the crimes provoked retribution, as, in very desperation, a few men, risking their own lives on the issue, took the law into their own hands and swept these monsters from the face of the earth.

It is not easy to forget such a tragedy, and it comes back most vividly when passing over the dark and bloody ground where it was enacted. As I remembered even the names of those who were actors in it, when we came back to Helena, and drove into the town, I said: "The man I want to see is Colonel Sanders," who was the leader of the Vigilantes, and was afterwards the first man to represent Montana in the Senate of the United States, and we drove straight to his door. At last I found my man. He received me with a hearty welcome that emboldened me to ask all sorts of questions; and leaving my friends to take their drive, I undertook the business (natural to my profession) of interviewing, to which he submitted with such docility that, not only as we sat in his hospitable home, but as we walked about the streets for two or three hours, we talked of little else but the early days of Montana. It is a long story, of which I can give only the substance, and this I will try to do as nearly as possible in his own words:

"When I first came to this country over thirty years ago (in 1863) Montana was without a government. There was not within five hundred miles a judge or a court to which a man could appeal for protection against the rough characters that always drift to the border. If there had been any pretence of administering justice, it would have been a mere form, since no jury would convict in the presence of men armed with shot-guns, so that violence ruled the country. This state of things grew worse and worse, till no man was safe. In a few cases, where men had been caught in the very act of robbery or murder, and were executed on the spot, just before they were swung off they made confessions that implicated many who had not been suspected before, so that we knew not whom to trust. A man's nearest neighbor might be his secret enemy; nobody knew what a day might bring forth."

"I never knew," said a gentle voice, that of the noble woman who shared his fortunes in this time of danger, "when my husband went out in the morning, whether he would return at night."

"At last," resumed the Colonel, "we grew desperate. It was better to die than to live in such a community. Society was dissolved, and we were thrown back upon ourselves for protection. There were a few of us who knew one another well enough to trust and be trusted,

and, meeting in secret, we bound ourselves by every tie
that could bind men together, to stand by one another
to the last. So was organized the famous band of Vigilantes. The first step was to seize the ringleaders, who
had been so daring and defiant that everybody knew
them, if they did not know the rank and file. If we
could, by a quick movement, seize them and disarm them,
their followers would be left without leaders, and be paralyzed. So we struck at the tall heads first. To those
who looked on from the outside, it seemed an amazing
piece of audacity, which would probably fail, when
those who had set themselves up as judges and executioners would have a swift shrift. The ringleaders were
not very much disturbed, for they saw many ways of
escape, but, when they found that the men of law and
order were in dead earnest, they took a more subdued
tone, and only asked for a fair trial! But the Vigilantes
knew too well what that meant—that it meant delay, with
all the chances of rescue and escape, or of a man on the
jury who would stand out against conviction. And so
when the case was proved (for the career of most of
these men was notorious), there was but one more step—
and that was execution! They did not have to wait for
a gallows; any tree in the forest would answer, and a
strong rope thrown round the limb of an Oregon fir
with the other end in the hands of a dozen strong men,
would quickly put an end to the career of the boldest
outlaw.

"These executions were not without danger, for we
knew well that in the crowd that gathered to see an execution there were many who were in sympathy with the
victims. But the Vigilantes took no risk, and came to
the scene armed to the teeth, so that if any man had

lifted a hand to interfere with the course of justice, he would have been shot down in an instant.

"Under the new rule of law and order the ranks of outlaws thinned out. The old villains, who boasted of the number of their murders, as an Indian carries his scalps as his trophies, saw that the game was up, and their last piece of bravado was to show that they were not afraid to die. One famous desperado, who had the rope round his neck, and saw another swinging in the air and making fearful struggles for release, instead of a word of pity for his comrade, who had come to such an end, could only shout, 'Kick away, old Jack, I'll be in hell with you in ten minutes!'"

"The most extraordinary case was that of a man who came from the East, and belonged to a respectable family, and bore a fair reputation. Strange as it may seem, I had accepted an invitation to dine with him at Thanksgiving (for even then we had to keep up an appearance of enjoying ourselves), for which he made great preparations, sending off four hundred miles for a turkey, for which he paid forty dollars in gold! It might have occurred to us that such a man must have plenty of money to spend, and got it in an easy way. But we did not stop to think of anything but to have a little gayety in the midst of so much to try our nerves; and, though it was a backwoods feast, we all made ourselves as merry as we could in those grim days. Imagine my amazement when, shortly after, a man who was standing on the scaffold made a full confession, in which he 'gave away' all his comrades; and among them—not only as a member of the gang, but as the ringleader, the man who plotted all the robberies, and whose hands were red with a dozen murders—was none other than the man who had entertained us on Thanksgiving Day! This confession was supplemented by evidence from without, so that there was no possible doubt in the case, and it became my duty to arrest the very man whose hospitality I had accepted but six weeks before!

"Never shall I forget the scene of his execution. It was in the winter, and at night, and yet it was not dark, as the moon was shining on the snow that covered the ground, when the Vigilantes took him to a place in the woods. Two others were to die with him, who begged piteously for the mercy they had never shown to others. 'If they could only have a little delay!' 'Only wait!' But the Vigilantes knew too well what possibilities there might be in the postponement for a single hour. After them came the leader, whose bravado oozed out of him as he came to his inevitable fate, and as his body swung in the cold winter wind, an end was put to the career of one of the most notorious villains in the whole catalogue of crime!"

Is this a harrowing tale to be told on the very spot where such scenes occurred? Yes, indeed, but the shedding of blood was the price of order and of liberty. Had not this league of men of law and order taken things into their own hands, Montana would not have been a place in which honest men and women could live.

After all this time of seizures and executions there was a great silence and a great calm all round the horizon. Montana, from being the hunting ground of robbers and cut-throats, was the most quiet and peaceable of all the Territories, and this city was the model town on the border. There was no violence in her streets. No man needed to lock his door, to guard against thieves. Even if a stranger should drop his purse in the streets, they said, no passer-by would pick it up, lest he should be thought to have stolen it. And thus, out of these terrible scenes came the reign of law, which made possible the creation of the beautiful city set on a hill, that bears the queenly name of Helena, and is the capital of Montana to-day.

CHAPTER XXI

THE YELLOWSTONE PARK

HERE beginneth another chapter of my story. We had crossed the continent, and were now recrossing it; and, if we had not measured half the distance, yet in that long dark Bozeman Tunnel, through which we passed yesterday, the highest point of which is over a mile above the level of the sea, we crossed the Continental Divide, and were now at the very bottom of the mountains.* As the descending grade had doubled our speed, we were literally flying, and the temptation was very great to keep up the pace, and still fly, as on the wings of the morning, over the plains to our Eastern home.

Why should we stop for a day or an hour? Will the eye never be satisfied with seeing? Does not the Bible tell us to turn off our eyes from beholding vanity? So I could have reasoned with myself, had not "a Peri standing at the gate" suddenly thrown it ajar, and given us a glimpse of something that could not be seen elsewhere in all the round world, after which I should as soon have thought of passing by the gates of heaven, as to turn away from such a wonderland when the gates stood open before us.

---

* "At Livingston the railroad (going westward) crosses the Yellowstone for the last time, and immediately begins the ascent of the first range of the Rocky Mountains."—*Arnold Hague.*

But the first approach did not promise much. Livingston, where the traveller leaves the Northern Pacific, is a place of little interest except as a railway station. Here we passed the night. In the morning I was up at an early hour, and, strolling out of the little town, came to a river that, like all mountain streams, was rushing swiftly over its bed. "What is this?" I asked of the first countryman. "The Yellowstone!" This was like coming on the sources of the Nile, for, like the great river of Africa, the Yellowstone is a stream of high birth and long descent, rising on the top of the mountains in a lake that is nearly eight thousand feet above the level of the sea (we shall see it by and by and sail over it), from which it starts on its career over a continent. If I were to drop a rubber ball into it, it would float down five hundred miles to the Missouri, and two thousand more to the Mississippi, and over a thousand more to the Gulf of Mexico—a course as long as that of the Nile from the lakes of Central Africa to the Mediterranean.

With this slight suggestion of great distances to whet our appetite for the vast and the wonderful, we leave Livingston, from which the Northern Pacific Company, that does everything for everybody in this region of the mid-continent, has built a side-road from its trunk line, fifty miles to Cinnabar. Here we say good-bye to railroads, and taking our seats in an old-fashioned stage-coach, begin to climb the hills. As soon as we cross the line of the Yellowstone Park, we see that we are in a public reservation. Though it was a part of the State of Wyoming, it belongs to the General Government, and is under the nation's care for protection. The roads, though winding through gorges, by rapid mountain streams, are laid out by government engineers, and built much more solidly than they could be by the few settlers scattered over hundreds of square miles. It was rather a lonely ride, for there can hardly be said to be any settled population, the only life that is passing being that of the parties coming and going. Our driver pointed out to us one old settler, a bald-headed eagle, that had built his nest on the top of a huge pillar of rock, from which he looked down, perchance with wonder or contempt, upon those who had dared to invade his domain.

Though it is but seven miles, it is a good hour and a half's pull before we reach the point where we wind round a cliff and come in sight of an open space, surrounded by a number of buildings, which, with the adjoining stables, show that they are the barracks of a cavalry post; while the flag flying over the largest of them indicates the official residence of the commanding officer. Here, driving round the open grounds, the coach reins up at the Mammoth Hot Springs Hotel.

A good hotel is a mark of civilization; and here we have it in a building as large as one of the great caravanserais at Saratoga, capable of holding several hundred guests, with a veranda six hundred feet long, on which the travellers gather in the summer evening to talk over the events of the day.

Hardly were we settled in our rooms before we had a call from Captain Anderson, to whom I had letters from the Secretary of the Interior and from General Schofield, commending us to his courtesies. He was full of kindness, but regretted that he had not the means of contributing as he would to our pleasure, inasmuch as almost his whole command had been ordered to different points along the railroad to protect stations and bridges and tunnels from the attacks of strikers. He had hardly men enough left to perform sentinel duty, and to fire the gun at sunrise and sunset. Those who were gone had taken their horses with them, which might be needed, in case of sudden alarm, to transport their riders to some threatened spot; so that he had hardly a team left with which to give us a drive of a few miles round the hotel. I thanked the gallant Captain for his kind intention, but assured him that his brave men were much better employed than in ministering to our pleasure, however agreeable such courtesies might be in more peaceful times.

The first inquiry of a stranger is for the Mammoth Hot Springs, which give name to the place, and these are not far to seek. They are not springs of running water, but simply the overflow of mineral substances that have been dissolved in the boiling caldron under the earth and forced upward through the fissures of the rocks, to be cooled in the upper air. Thus the world is turned inside out, and the result is a revelation. We have read of the gems which

"The dark, unfathomed caves of ocean bear,"

but here the very rocks under our feet conceal bits of color that, when brought out, shine like the topaz and the emerald; and when these varied tints are spread over a surface covering many acres, causing them to glisten with all the colors of the rainbow, it is impossible to conceive of anything more exquisite. Nature puts on her beautiful garments, now arraying herself in snowy white, now in sky blue, and now in darker colors, as if suddenly clouds had come over the sky. The effect is strange and startling, and we can hardly help giving a mystic significance to the scene when on a large background of dark or white we see great splashes of red, as if nature had received some deadly wound, and were sweating great drops of blood!

Such a pricking of the veins and arteries of the hard and solid globe, we believe, has no parallel. A few years since, similar "terraces" were discovered in New Zealand, which were the subject of curious observation by all the men of science who visited the antipodes; but the most wonderful of these, the White Terrace, has since been destroyed by an earthquake, so that the phenomenon here is probably the most remarkable of its kind in the world.

In the hotel there is always a crowd of strangers from all parts of the country, among whom are many persons of distinction. It was good to see the face of that grand old soldier, ex-Governor Beaver, of Pennsylvania, in company with General Hastings, who had just been nominated for that high office. He has since been elected by an overwhelming majority.

Another gentleman whom we met here for the first time was Mr. Thomas F. Oakes, late President, and now Receiver, of the Northern Pacific Railroad. I am coming to look upon the controllers of our great railroads as among the most important men in the country, both in the possession of power, and in the capacity to wield it. To manage a railroad system extending over hundreds or thousands of miles requires as much executive ability as to be the governor of a State or Secretary of the Treasury. Of this class of men is Mr. Oakes. A New Englander by birth, he has the best blood of old Massachusetts in his veins. A graduate of Boston schools, he left them to enter the army; and when the war was over, he, like so many officers of rank, turned his knowledge of engineer-

MAMMOTH HOT SPRINGS.

ing to the creation and equipment of those great highways that were beginning to stretch out their long arms across the continent. He has been connected with the Northern Pacific for many years, and was now on a tour of inspection of all its western connections, in the course of which he turned in hither for a few days, and thus it was our good fortune to meet him; and as we were for a week driving over the same roads, and resting at the same hotels, we were often in his company, and to his kindness and courtesy we owe much of the pleasure of our visit to the Yellowstone Park.

The next morning the sunrise gun startled us, like the blast of a bugle, and there was mustering in hot haste, as the chariots of war were set in battle array. For chariots put stout coaches, built for mountain roads, of which half a dozen rolled up to the broad veranda, to take on board the different parties. I was to have the special privilege of sitting on the box, from which I could look out on all sides at once, and take in the full glory of the mountains. But just as I was about to take possession, I heard a voice beside me, "Uncle, would you mind if I should take your seat beside the driver?" "Would you mind?" Who could stand such pleading as that? "Why yes, my dear child, of course you can have it. But do be careful, for you know the danger!" I was the more anxious because the high altitude had already caused her head to swim. "Sit far back in the seat, and hold fast to the hand-rail for support, lest any jolt in going down the mountain should throw you over the board and under the horses' feet!"

With this caution I felt partly assured, but still kept putting my head out of the windows to see if all was right. But I fear that my fatherly warnings were soon forgotten; for we had driven but a mile or two, when the meek and obedient little miss turned quietly to the driver and asked *if she might take the reins!* He thought it more prudent to keep them in his own hands till we had passed over the steepest ascents and descents; but as soon as we struck a more level road, he yielded them gracefully, and she, crossing the reins so as to give her easy control of her four-in-hand, kept the well-trained horses on a good round trot for a couple of hours without the slightest indication of fear or weariness.

This first day's drive is pleasantly relieved by an hour's stop at Norris, or "Larry's," a sort of camp in the woods, where parties coming and going meet to take lunch and exchange their experiences. Here we saw our first geyser, which, of course, was an object of wonder, though put out of sight by what we were to see afterwards, and indeed before the close of the day, at the Fountain Geyser Basin, which we reached in the afternoon. Here is a whole field of geysers, that boil and bubble, and fume and sputter, and toss their spray into the air.

It is one of the felicities of travelling in the Yellowstone Park, that, while one has all the romance of a life in the woods, he has at the same time the comforts of civilization. There is no need of roughing it. Although the Park is sixty-five miles long by fifty-five wide, it is so mapped out that inside of a week—indeed, in five days—he can make the circuit of all the points of greatest interest, travelling over good roads, and sleep every night in a clean bed. But if one wishes to take it more leisurely, there are camping parties that get up an excursion by themselves, going on their own hook, carrying their own provisions, and pitching their tents under the trees. In this way they wander about at will, and have a good time at very little expense.

But there is one class of pleasure seekers for whom this is *not* the place—those who are after sport. This is not a hunting ground. Fishing is permitted, though only with hook and line, but not hunting. Indeed, this is the one thing that is forbidden, and forbidden under penalty of the law. The reason for this is obvious. One object of setting aside the Park is to have a national preserve for the elk and the buffalo, and other animals that are native to our plains and our mountains, but that are in danger of becoming extinct. Already the buffaloes that once covered the Western prairies are exterminated. Here there is a herd of three or four hundred that are kept in this preserve in the hope of increase, that there may be at least a remnant of these native Americans. Lest any of them should be shot, no man is allowed to bring a gun into the Park. If he pleads innocent intentions, and only wishes to have it when he goes away, he is required to give security for his good behavior in having the trigger strapped and sealed so that he cannot fire it off; and if he breaks his faith, his gun is taken from him and he is arrested. How quickly the law takes him in hand, I saw last night at the Hot Springs Hotel, when I perceived a stir in the hall, occasioned by a man's showing himself who, some months since, had shot ten or a dozen buffaloes. He was at once tapped on the shoulder and marched over to the guard house.

Thus watched over by good angels, this Park is the paradise of dumb animals, and indeed of all God's creatures, except where man has smitten it with a curse. Strange as it may seem, it is said by old woodsmen and hunters that the elk and the buffalo know that they are under a kind of protection. This I did not believe at first, and don't quite believe it now; but they say that if any of the herds stray across the border, and come within the range of the hunter, and hear the crack of a rifle, they start in a wild stampede for the Park, and stop not till they are within the pale of safety. And not only elk and buffalo, but wild animals grow tame. Man and beast have renounced hostilities, and are brought into friendly relations. Even bears, that are so much of a terror to settlers in the woods, have joined the peace society, and if they do not "eat straw like the ox," yet they seem so far domesticated as to cease to be objects of fear or of danger. We were told how they come about the houses and make themselves at home. To be sure, this devotion to a domestic life is not altogether disinterested, for they are, like Tammany politicians, after the pickings and stealings, and, like the said politicians again, they have sensitive nostrils to tell them where to find what they are after. If there has been a big dinner at a hotel, they snuff the fragrance from afar, and it is a temptation that no bear's virtue can resist. And so at nightfall they come out of the woods, and begin to snuff round the kitchen, and put their noses into the tubs which contain the refuse of the feast.

At the Fountain Hotel, where we spent the first night, they told us the bears were such frequent visitors that they did not take any notice of them. "Why, only last night," said one of the boys, "we had quite a 'posse' of them. Big and little, old bears and cubs, I counted thirteen! They came round to the kitchen behind the house, and poked into everything, and had lots of fun!" But a bird in the hand is worth two in the bush, and a bear that I see with my own eyes is worth a dozen that I hear about. So I answered: "You say you had a dozen last night; show me one!" "Well," said the boy, apparently chagrined that I did not quite trust him, "there is one out in the lot now!" "Where is he?" I cried; "show him to me!" Whereupon he led the way across the field in the rear of the house to the edge of the wood, and sure enough there stood a huge cinnamon bear, nosing among some tin cans for the remnants of delicacies that might still be toothsome to his royal taste. He did not show any fierceness at our appearance, but now and then raised his head and looked us in the face. Of course, if he had taken a step towards us, we should have found discretion the better part of valor, but as he did not move, we plucked up courage to advance a little nearer, followed, at a safe distance, by stragglers from the hotel; whereupon Bruin, instead of charging upon us, turned his huge bulk, and moved off, not rapidly, but with proper dignity, back into the woods and partly up the hill. But he was a peaceable old gentleman, for he walked right into a pasture where the cows were grazing, that did not even raise their heads, but went on cropping the grass. They let the bear alone, and he let them alone! As to "the humans" on the other side of the fence, if the bear had any thoughts about it, no doubt it was that we were very uncivil to intrude upon his domain. But, as we did not attempt active hostilities, he, like the king of Spain, having marched up the hill, now marched down again, and was soon engaged in what is one great duty of bears as well as of men, eating his supper; whereupon Mabel and I, like two foolish children, real "Babes in the Wood," ran towards him; Of course, if he had stood his ground, or moved a single step towards us, we should have been frightened out of our wits and run for dear life. But, lo! the monster once more "turned tail," and retreated into the forest, where, for obvious reasons, we did not care to pursue the subject! Of course, we were immensely set up by our victory, though it suggested to me a moral reflection, that what is called victory is not always owing to the courage of the assailant, but quite as often to the cowardice of his opponent! It would have been more in accordance with poetical justice if the bear had turned on the "Babes in the Wood" and torn them in pieces; though in that case, to complete the tragic history, it would have been necessary that the robins should come and cover the babes with the leaves of the forest!

CHAPTER XXII

THE GEYSERS.

It was the last day of July, when the heat of summer not only quivered in the upper air, but dropped down into the cool depths of the woods. But this warmth only made the shade more grateful, and through the lights and shadows we wound our way, enjoying again the indescribable charm of a drive through the primeval forest. But the great event of the day was to be a full view of the geysers, of which we had a first sight at the Lower Geyser Basin, and now were to have the culmination. An hour's drive brought us to the Excelsior, a name that describes its past glory rather than its present performance. Indeed, it is now a cluster of hot springs and bubbling pools, that spread over what is called Hell's Half-Acre. This is a bad name to give to any portion of God's earth, as if it were accursed; but I am afraid there was a time when it deserved it, when the evil spirit confined in the caverns below broke loose, and burst its bars asunder, and threw up a mighty column two hundred and fifty feet into the air, which descended like molten lava, destroying everything it touched, like an eruption of Vesuvius. It did not, indeed, set fire to cities like Pompeii and Herculaneum, but it made the waters boil like a pot, turning the Firehole River into a steaming caldron, that was instant death to man or beast that put so much as a foot into the scalding pool. **While such eruptions lasted, this geyser** was not only Excelsior, but stood **alone, as a** display of the **forces that are at** work in the **interior** of the globe. But the very intensity of the explosion exhausted its **force, so that after** a few months of rage and fury, the old Excelsior sank down into quietness, and now is a name of terror to the world only because of its former greatness.

In the study **of nature it is** better to go from the dead to the living than from the living to the dead, and so **we** are kept in pleased expectancy as we pass from the field **of** a spent geyser, which is like a burnt-out volcano, **to** the field of a great number that are in full activity, for **such is** the Upper Geyser Basin. Here the under-world **is all alive.** The hammer of Vulcan is ever ringing in the cavern in which he forges his thunderbolts, and if it **be not fire** and smoke **that** issue from the earth, there is **a** constant letting **off of** steam, with **a** throwing up of great columns, like water-spouts in the ocean, the signs and proofs of the tremendous forces that are working far down in this terrestrial sphere. As we come into the basin **which** is the field of action, we find the geysers increase in number and in variety. No two are alike. Each has an individuality **of its own, as it** has its peculiar formation. Here, for example, is the Castle, which has the figure of a small fortress, surrounded by walls, to which is given an addition to its military appearance by the presence of a soldier, who keeps guard that visitors **do not throw** substances into it that might so mix with the elements below as to cause a dangerous explosion.

As some of the geysers are majestic in size, others are small in comparison. These I call young geysers, that have not yet come to man's estate, but that, like precocious children, are eager to show themselves, and so put their heads out of the ground, and fume and sputter as if they were of some importance, as indeed they would be if they were not overshadowed by the monarchs of that nether-world to which they belong.

The great field of observation of the geysers is a plateau that has been formed by the overflow of the many that are in constant action. It is a somewhat slippery surface over which we picked our way, observing the differing size and shapes which give names to the more noted among them. Now the incrustations have grown up into something like a Beehive. Again it is a Lion Couchant, not far from whose noble form is that of the Lioness; and a little distance from their father and mother is an interesting group of young lions, mere cubs, but which have a lively appearance that gives promise of the full leonine stature to which they may grow.

The effect of so many geysers going off at once is not unlike that at sea when a shoal of porpoises come round a ship, leaping and spouting, and follow in the long track behind. Or, to take a more grave and clerical illustration, as I looked round on this great assembly that was all alive and somewhat vociferous, it seemed to me that I was in a camp-meeting, that was in such a state of excitement that half of those present rose to speak at once, while those who were trying to keep silent could not altogether hold their peace, but responded, now with groans, and now with amens and hallelujahs! It was a thoroughly Methodist congregation, and yet, among so many effervescent brethren, it was gratifying to see one grand old Presbyterian, and he the patriarch of them all, who, because of his regularity and uniformity, has been christened Old Faithful. I call him a Presbyterian, because he is always on time; you always know where to find him. As for the common run of geysers, they come at all hours, with or without warning; and behave in such an irregular way, breaking out in spots, and doing the most unexpected things, that they are not to be depended upon. But Old Faithful comes and goes by the clock. It is said of the old Puritan divines that they preached with an hour-glass on the pulpit, and when the sands were run out, instead of letting the sermon run out also, simply turned the glass upside down, with the cheering exhortation, "Now, brethren, let us take another hour!" Old Faithful requires a little more time to get his "second wind," but at the end of sixty-five minutes exactly, he speaks in a tone that all must hear.

Knowing his regular habits, the congregation comes together at the appointed hour, where, in front of the pulpit, at a safe distance, is a rude bench, such as one may find at a camp-meeting in the woods. I would not call it a "mourners' bench," nor an "anxious seat," though it is certainly occupied by those who are in a lively state of expectancy, both as listeners and spectators.

For my part, I did not sit at all, but walking up the slippery mound formed by the overflow of the geyser, leaned over the edge and looked down the monster's throat. There was not much to see, and herein I was disappointed, for I had imagined that the greatest of the geysers would speak through a mighty trumpet; that his throat, if not quite like the crater of a volcano, would at least be a large aperture, massive and well rounded, like a well bored by Titans into the heart of the earth. And the walls must be smooth, for, as the waters wear away stones, the rocks must be polished like marble by the constant rush from below. But, instead of that, I saw only black and jagged projections, which, if they had ever been smoothed, had been rent again by fresh explosions, so that they were still blasted and torn.

It was not yet sermon time, and the preacher was not quite ready to begin, but he had already great wrestlings of heart, and was clearing his throat to give them utterance. We heard rumblings and mutterings, and once or twice I felt a splash in my face that would have scalded me to the bone had it not been instantly cooled by exposure to the air. These little love taps I did not mind, but I had been all the time keeping what a sailor would call his "weather eye" out for anything more serious, and now did not stand on the order of my going, but retired with more haste than dignity.

Then we heard the thunder of his voice. It was not, indeed, like a thunder-clap, sharp and startling as the crack of doom, but more like the inrolling of the sea, with the foaming crest of the wave riding in advance to tell of the mighty billow that is behind. When this came in its strength, it threw, a hundred and fifty feet in the air, a column of water that must have been tons in weight, but that was hurled upward with such velocity that it had an airy lightness, and, broadening at the top, fell in a shower of spray all around. And then with what grace the majestic form withdrew from the scene! It did not collapse, nor fall flat, but retired like some spirit of the air, lowering itself, not instantaneously, but by degrees, stooping and rising again, as some royal personage who, after giving audience to his court, retires, bowing to the right and left, and is gone.

So transcendent was the beauty of the scene, that it seemed as if one could never weary of it, and, as we stayed here till the next day, I saw it repeatedly. If it could be more beautiful at one time than another, perhaps the most wonderful display that I witnessed was the next morning a little after sunrise. I had risen early for the purpose, and taken a seat at a window which looked right toward Old Faithful, but a few rods distant, where I could keep my eye on him even while I was writing, and my ear too, to hear his first mutterings; and the moment I caught the sound I dropped everything, and in an instant was all eye and ear for but one object. As I was the only person up in the hotel, except the servants, he gave this performance for me alone, and certainly he never played his part more to perfection. In this he was helped by the new-risen sun, whose rays shot through the veil of mist that hung in the sky. That sunlight was more than a bow in the cloud; it was as if the Divine Presence itself was throned on the cloud, shedding light and joy and hope on the new-born world.

It is hard to come down from this mount of vision to mere science—which to most observers of nature is mere materialism. But we cannot help asking, What do these geysers, with their attendant phenomena, reveal to us in regard to the constitution of our globe? Is it solid? Or is it hollow? If the latter, is there any life in its interior? Or do the elements alone—fire and water and gravitation—have universal sway? Are there "waters under the earth"? Is there an ocean that sweeps from pole to pole, rolling and resounding where there is no eye to see and no ear to hear?

These questions are not new; they have exercised the minds of men for ages; and the less men knew about this great mystery, the more they gave way to their imaginations. In the ancient mythology there was an under-world, that was the place of departed spirits, who inhabited "the shades," and, recalling their past evil lives, were filled with remorse, as they wandered on the "dark Plutonian shore."

Even Christian theology has been invaded by these fancies, and the interior of the earth has been thought to be the abode of the damned, where the universal gloom, the darkness that may be felt, is but the outward token of their mental state—their horror and despair. All these are subjects on which it is much easier to ask questions than to answer them; and into this realm of darkness I seek not to explore.

CHAPTER XXIII

THE LAKE AND THE RIVER

The next morning I sat for more than two hours at the window writing, and keeping watch of Old Faithful, who gave two grand performances for my sole benefit. But he was not the only object of wonder or curiosity. My attention was divided between the great geyser, and looking for a bear who had taken up his quarters at the hotel. He was not an old acquaintance, as he had come from the woods only a week or two before, but was of such a domestic turn of mind that he made himself at home anywhere, whether "under the greenwood tree," or under a house or a barn. But in coming to abide with men, he did not submit to be a servant under bondage, to be confined in a cage, or held by a chain; but was a free and independent citizen, free in all his goings out and comings in, as if he took the place of a faithful old servitor, who has earned the right to have his own way; to have the run of the kitchen, or what was thrown out from the kitchen; and in all respects to live as a pensioner of the family.

Presenting himself in this inoffensive manner, it was but a natural return of good will that no one interfered with the new visitor. He came and went with the freedom of an honored guest. Nobody troubled him; no boys threw stones at him; nobody called him bad names, as if he were a tramp or a vagabond. He was a decent member of society, who went on the principle of live and let live. Like a sensible old gentleman, he spent a good deal of his time in sleep. But asleep or awake he was not looked upon as an intruder or a beggar, but as a privileged member of the household.

What a picture of primeval innocence and peace! I was curious to see this addition to the family, and asked "Where is he?" with vague suspicions that he might be a myth. But "No, no," said the innkeeper; "by and by he will make his appearance. Perhaps he is here *now!*" With that he went about the house, looking underneath it, till suddenly he exclaimed, "Why, there he is!" I was down on my knees in an instant, and sure enough, right under the floor, indeed under my very feet, where I had been writing, was what might be a bear or a buffalo. The next thing was to stir him up, and make him show himself. The master of the house tried to poke him with a stick, but had not one long enough. Then he threw stones at him. But the thick brown hair was proof against stones, and the burly old creature slept on with proper contempt of the pygmies that were trying to disturb his repose. I confess I rather respected him for his royal indifference to his puny assailants. The landlord apologized for his want of deference to his visitors, but explained it thus: "The old fellow takes his time about everything. He has probably been off in the woods to visit his family, to see Mrs. Bear and his children or grandchildren, and is now a little tired. By and by he will wake up and feel hungry, and then he will come round to the door for his breakfast, which he will take from our hands as if he were a Newfoundland dog."

This was a pretty story, and my happiness would have been complete if the "old fellow" had only waked up a little sooner, and I could have looked squarely in his honest face, and patted him and petted him, stroking his long hair, and having him eat out of my hand, which would have been a beautiful sign of the brotherhood of man with what we are pleased to call the lower creatures.

When it came to bidding good-by to the geysers, and continuing our excursion through the Park, I found that a new state of things was developed. My junior partner had awakened to find herself famous. Her handling of the reins had given her a reputation among the coach drivers. Even Mr. Huntley (who is in the Park what in England, in the royal household, would be called Master of the Horse) looked upon her with a new respect, and invited her to ride in a light carriage, with a pair of spirited horses that he would trust to no one but himself; to which I assented, thinking that he might allow her to please herself with the idea that she was driving for a mile or two along the level road, while the real security was in his own strong hands.

When our youthful charioteer (whom, to tell the truth, I had looked upon as rather ornamental than useful) was thus transferred, I was restored to the place on the box that was originally designed for me, where I took my seat beside a driver who was quite a character; who not only knew every mile of the road, every twist and turn, every rock and cliff, every stream and waterfall, but who had roughed it on the border for years, and had a life that was not without incident. He had been up and down the Pacific Coast; had visited Alaska, and crossed the mountains by the Indian trail to the valley of the Yukon, allured by the marvellous tales of gold, which he found half true; but the hope of riches was abated by the fact that the country is for three-quarters of the year covered with snow, during which the miners have to hibernate. And so he came back a poorer as well as a sadder and a wiser man. But his bad luck did not sour his temper, nor make him curse the world. He took it all with a rough backwoods philosophy, and told the story of his experiences and adventures with a dry mother-wit that was very entertaining. For a day in a "mountain land" one could not ask a better fellow to be his companion and guide than Billy Maine.

The ride through the woods has a variety which gives it a constant novelty and interest. It is not all one dense, impenetrable forest, but here and there are great openings, where giant trees stand alone, as in an English park. Now and then the road comes to the verge of high cliffs. At one point we drew up by the roadside, and stepped out upon a pile of rocks, that towered above a gorge that it made my head swim even to look down upon.

Of course our progress was slow, because it was all ups and downs. Twice we crossed the Continental Divide, from the Atlantic slope to the Pacific, and back again. In climbing upward, Billy, like the good and careful driver that he is, was very gentle to his horses, never cracking the whip, or urging them to speed. But when at last he reached the summit, and had given them a good breathing spell, he touched them lightly, saying, "Now we must make up for lost time," and the stalwart team responded as one that knew its master. First it was a gentle trot, but soon grew faster and faster, till we swung round the turns in the road with a swiftness that made me take firm grasp of the hand-rail lest I should be thrown from my perch over upon the tops of the trees that covered the mountain side.

But no sense of danger could make us insensible to the sublimity of the scene that opened before us as we crossed the Divide for the second time. Away over the tops of the trees, over the sea of mountains, we caught sight of another sea, embosomed in these mighty solitudes, and yet itself so high that it seemed almost as if it belonged to some other world than ours. This language is hardly extravagant when it is considered that in altitude it stands alone in North America, as there is no other body of water at once so large and so high, being twenty miles long and sixteen miles broad, and nearly eight thousand feet above the level of the sea! But it is not, as represented in some of the guide books, the highest in the world. Lake Titicaca, in Peru, up in the Andes, is twelve thousand eight hundred feet above sea level, and eighty miles long and forty broad! It is also near a city of five thousand inhabitants, and is navigated.

But descending to the shore, we find that the sea— which is none other than the Yellowstone Lake—has, in spite of its elevation, its familiar surroundings. Here is a sort of camp, with the tents pitched, where we can sit, as it were, under the palm trees, and take our rest and refreshment, with a pebbled beach leading down to the water, where a little steamboat is waiting to take us down the lake.

Of course, my first anxiety was for my child, who had been whirled over the mountains with more speed than suited my fancy for a sober Presbyterian gait. But I felt assured that no accident could happen with the

Master of the Horse in command. Imagine my surprise to hear him say, "I never touched the reins!" "And you dared to trust your life, going up and down these mountains for nineteen miles, to that child!" He had told me that no woman had ever driven his "crack team" except his wife, who, having lived on a ranche in the beautiful Gallatin Valley, had had the training that one gets on the great plains of Montana, and could almost drive a wild buffalo. "Next to her," he said, "your niece is the best woman driver I ever saw. She holds the reins beautifully." And then he went on to explain, with the enthusiasm of an artist, just how she held them. "She does not fret the horses, but gives them their freedom, while she keeps them firmly in hand." To all this I listened with a mixed feeling of pleasure and of pain—pain that she should be a child no more. Oh, dear! oh, dear! to think that my poor little chicken, that was hardly out of the hen-coop, should take to herself the airs of womanhood, and even now turn back her soft, tender, and pitying eyes on her fond old uncle!

This sober reflection was somewhat relieved by the change from the carriage to the boat, where we saw before us what might have been one of the Swiss lakes, embosomed in some deep Alpine valley. But there is one difference—our Alpine lake is not only embosomed among the mountains, but throned above the mountains. If Mount Washington were planted in this very spot the waves would not only roll over him and bury him out of sight, but only deep-sea soundings could touch the tallest pine upon his lofty head. This single fact increased our respect for our American lake, albeit it is little known even among ourselves, and almost unknown to the rest of the world. And when we came to sail over it, and I thought of these heights and depths, a strange feeling came over me (perhaps it was the effect of imagination) that, as we were breathing a higher atmosphere than that of the world below, so all our surroundings were on a higher plane; the very clouds hung lower, and the vault above came nearer, until we were literally floating between the earth and sky.

But no nearness to heaven could abate the gayety of such a party as ours, and the group that gathered on deck, perhaps exhilarated by the lighter and purer air of this high altitude, was in a state of joyous excitement; while the young lady, who in the morning had shown herself such a whip, was now invited into the pilot-house, where the sailor at the wheel was so much pleased by her presence that he gallantly asked her to take his place, so that for an hour, although he stood by her and told her in what direction to steer, her hand guided the boat to the entire satisfaction of her superior officer; and indeed I think he would have been willing to take her as a pupil in his profession. Nor would that have been a useless accomplishment. Boating is by no means an unwomanly exercise. A little knowledge of how to turn a wheel or a tiller, or to use the oar, might save a young woman from panic in case of sudden danger, and perchance enable her to save her own life and the lives of others.

As we sailed down the lake, the distant mountains came nearer, and islands lifted their heads, as in the Italian lakes, to give the relief of variety to the scene. Rounding one of these islands to a sheltered spot, we drew alongside a pier and walked ashore, and up two or three flights of steps to a hotel beautifully situated, and whose appointments, if not as luxurious and extravagant as those of our Eastern watering-places, were, considering that we were in the mountains and far from civilization, all that could be desired.

But the day was not over; indeed, for some of our fellow-tourists, its greatest excitement was now to begin; for at this end of the lake it empties into the Yellowstone River, and this is the very place where the salmon-trout most do congregate. I could hardly understand the fascination of this sport till I saw the eagerness of some of our party to throw themselves into boats, and push off to the fishing ground. Mr. Huntley took his companion of the mountain drive in one boat, and I followed in another, in which sat the most expert fisherman in these waters, who had once caught—not in a net, mind you, but with hook and line—two hundred and fifty trout in one day! Now, having the glamour of this great achievement before my eyes, and fully expecting to see it repeated, I reasoned that, even though I was a silent partner in this new enterprise, yet the average for us both would be very high. Alas for my hopes, hardly had my friend begun to draw in the little beauties, before his rod broke, and he had to send back to the hotel, a mile away, for another! While waiting for his return, we ran the skiff on the beach, and, sitting on the soft warm sand, recalled old times in the history of this midcontinent. My companion had come to Montana at an early day, and, as one of the Vigilantes, had taken an active part in exterminating the robbers and murderers who infested the country. Of those scenes he could say, "All of which I saw, and part of which I was." In these tales of the border there is to me a terrible fascination, and I listened with eager attention, till the messenger returned with the new rod that was to work a miracle of fishes before the sun went down; and as I was no longer ambitious to divide the honors, I took the path along the shore back to the hotel, delighted not only with the Alpine scenery on every side, but, not least of all, to see the tents in the woods, which indicated the presence of soldiers, to insure protection alike to the Park itself, and to strangers who wander amid these solitudes. Even nature loses its charm when invaded by savagery and barbarism, and I felt grateful both to God and to my country, that here the spirit of lawlessness had been subdued; and that the lakes and mountains, so attractive by all their grandeur and their beauty, were the abodes of quietness and peace.

CHAPTER XXIV

THE CAÑON OF THE YELLOWSTONE

"THE Cañon of the Yellowstone is the greatest thing on earth!" This would have been putting it rather strong even for a sentimental traveller, who goes into raptures on the slightest occasion, and indulges in every extravagance of language. But more surprising was it from a grim soldier, who is not wont to be overawed by anything in nature or in war; but stands unmoved by the roar of the cataract as by the noise of the captains and the shouting. So when Captain Anderson, who had lived, as it were, in sight of the cañon for years—seeing it in summer and in winter, by day and by night—said to me, "It is the greatest thing on earth," it was what Dick Swiveller would have called "an unmitigated staggerer"; so that I was in some perturbation of mind, and set out this morning with an anticipation such as I had not had since that memorable night on the desert, when I was looking to see the sun rise on Mount Sinai.

But it is better not to rush into such a presence lightly or unadvisedly, but to linger a little on the way. Nature has prepared a fitting approach along the banks of the Yellowstone River, which comes out of the lake with the swiftness of the arrowy Rhone as it issues from the Lake of Geneva. As if to run a race with it, the light carriage that came over the mountains yesterday at such speed, now swept by us (with the reins in the hands of the same fearless driver) like the wind. But we were in no haste, and not only drove very slowly, but stopped several times and got out to stroll along under the trees that hang over the stream, like the willows by the rivers of Babylon. How beautiful it all was on this summer morning! As the roots of the trees reach out into the water, they form little pools that are more quiet than the rushing stream, and here the trout collect in shoals that would excite the enthusiasm of sportsmen. I am glad we had none of them with us, or if there were, that there was no time to show their skill with the rod and reel. I did not feel so yesterday, because I did not see the little creatures so clearly in the deep waters of the lake; but now that they are close under my eye, and I can see their exquisite beauty of form and color, it seems a wanton cruelty to destroy them just for the pleasure of destruction. I was not made for a sportsman, for really I could never see the sport in the angling of fishes, any more than in the shooting of birds!

What sort of a man is he who can find pleasure in shooting robins? Up in the hills where I have my summer home, I count the robins that come to us a part of the family. They are the first harbingers of spring. Hardly has the snow melted under the hill, before their soft notes tell us that the winter is over and gone. It is one of the delights of summer to see them hopping about the lawn, and drinking out of the fountain. We love to have them build their nests in the trees, or under the eaves; and to hear their bird notes, that are so soothing, as they seem to sing only of love and peace. If I were to take the life of one of these dainty creatures,

I should have a feeling of shame that would haunt me for weeks.

What the robins are in the air, the trout are in the river—creatures that are born to live in the sunshine, which penetrates even their watery realm, and not to die for the mere pleasure of their human destroyer. I do not object to fishing when it is for food, for the support of life; but when it is merely to show one's skill in whirling them into the air dangling at the end of a hook, I prefer to take my pleasure in some other way. It did not seem quite so yesterday, when the sufferers were out of sight; but here in these shallow waters, where I can almost touch them with my hand, they are so full of life and happiness that I should feel as if I were guilty of wanton cruelty if, for the mere excitement of a moment, I were to put an end to their joyous existence.

When we resumed our journey I changed places with a lady from Philadelphia, who was of our party, giving her the seat on the box, and taking her seat inside. If the former has some advantages, the latter is by no means to be despised, for a lumbering old coach is "as easy as an old shoe," and, as it swings on its leather hinges, one feels as if he were rocked in the cradle of the deep. And what a spacious interior it has! If it be not quite as big as a small house, it has a generous and hospitable look, as if it welcomed all comers, and could make room for all. And as the curtains are rolled up, we can see on both sides. It may be that Louis the Fourteenth, riding in his state coach, felt more grand than we, but I do not believe he was half as happy, as he was not half so free from care. And for the outlook, how puny and insignificant are the gardens of Versailles beside the wonders of the Yellowstone Park! Take it

16

all together, an ordinary traveller who "wants but little here below," should, on such a heavenly day as this, be more than satisfied.

In changing seats, I was sorry to lose the company of Billy Maine, but in his place we had old Dutch Louis, who was not less of a character. A German by birth, he had come to this country when a young man, and, when the war came on, enlisted in the army, and fought under Grant at Donelson and Shiloh and Vicksburg, and was with Sherman in his march to Atlanta. After the war was over, it was quite in the course of things that an old soldier, who had lived so long in the camp, should drift off to the Far West, and become a backwoodsman. In this new life he became a hunter and trapper, and learned all the ways of the forest, in which he acquired a good deal of "horse sense," and picked up a few jokes, which serve him on all occasions. We came across him first at the Mammoth Hot Springs. He showed us over the Terraces, where everything is so incrusted with lime that it seems as if water were turned into stone, upon which old Louis remarked solemnly that the absence of birds was accounted for by the fact that there could be no young ducks, since the old ducks laid hard-boiled eggs! Of course, nobody stops to analyze such wit. If it raises a laugh it answers its purpose, and it matters not if it be repeated to new-comers a dozen times a day. But, withal, the old fellow was a good guide, and nothing escaped his observation. "Look at that tree!" he said, pointing to an old dead trunk by the roadside. "You see the black mass in the crotch. It is an eagle's nest; yet not the bald eagle of the mountains, but the osprey, that feeds on fish, of which he finds an abundant supply in the lake."

We had left the geysers behind the day before, and had only one to-day, and that hardly worthy of the name, since its effervescence was not of pure water thrown up in shining columns, and falling in a shower of spray, but was simply a boiling pot of mud. The Mud Geyser is its name. I have heard of throwing mud in political disputes, and (to our shame be it said) sometimes in religious controversy, but really I thought that nature was above such a degradation. But here the black earth boils and bubbles, turning up a mass that might be the overflowing of the pit.

But all such impressions are forgotten as we come along the bank of the river, and find its current growing fast and furious, as it rushes on with increasing roar, like the rapids of Niagara, before it takes the final plunge.

It was a little after noon when we reined up at the Grand Cañon Hotel, and hardly was the dinner ended when wagons were brought round to the door to take us to Inspiration Point, which is nearly two miles away. This is no great matter for a mountain climber, or even a good pedestrian. But those who are weak in the knees or short of breath had better reserve what little strength they have for the moment when it is most needed. Old Louis put it very neatly when he said of the place of observation that "it was Inspiration Point, but if you walked it was Perspiration Point!" Not caring to waste either muscle or nerve, we let the horses take the first strain, and were soon winding through the deep woods, till we reached the cliffs, where we rode along a path which seemed perilously near to the edge, from which we could have sprung from the carriage and fallen upon the rocks hundreds of feet below.

At last we came to a stop under the trees, where the branches over our head made a cool shade, while the fallen leaves spread a soft carpet under our feet. From this safe eyry we had to advance but a few feet to stand on Inspiration Point, a huge pinnacle of rock, that stands out from the great wall of the cliff like a column that in time of war would be surmounted by a flagstaff, or signal, that could be seen for miles up and down the cañon. It is approached by a narrow (and I thought rather slippery) ridge, where I should wish to step very slowly and cautiously, even if I did not take off my shoes from my feet as if it were holy ground.

Although we were a gay and merry company, that in most cases were " up to anything," I observed that there was a little hesitation in rushing out on the place of " Inspiration." Or, to put it more gently, we deferred to one another, each willing to give precedence to a fellow-traveller. It was quite touching to observe the fine courtesy as one and another drew back to let somebody else lead the way!

In truth, it is enough to try the nerves of any one unaccustomed to great heights, to place his frail humanity on a needle point that stands so high in air that there is but a step between him and death. Men of powerful physique are not always sure of their own steadiness. A few weeks before our visit Mr. Hoke Smith, the Secretary of the Interior, had made a visit to the Yellowstone Park, and, though he is a man of giant frame, he told me that he could not trust himself to venture out on Inspiration Point.

But two or three of our party advanced with an air of confidence, and stood on the very verge of the precipice. Among these was my little maiden, who would venture anywhere, though she confessed to me afterwards (not, I am sorry to say, with the proper degree of humiliation) that she was badly frightened, but that she "was determined to do it if she died for it!"

As for her old uncle, of course it was from pure modesty that he kept in the background, walking with slow and solemn step, as if he were going up to a mount of sacrifice, and finally venturing but half way.

He came back to the hotel disappointed—not with the Cañon nor Inspiration Point, but with himself—that he had come to see the greatest thing on earth, and been kept back from a full open vision by his own nervousness. He would see it again with unshaken nerves and unshrinking feet, and so determined to prolong his visit to another day.

We did not lose the Cañon when we left the woods; it followed us everywhere. Our rooms in the hotel overlooked it. I do not mean that they looked down into it, for which it would have been necessary to make a nearer approach, but that they looked across the deep gorge in which it lies buried.

With a waterfall thus in sight and in hearing, we could not forget it, and the first thing the next morning was to visit both the Upper and the Lower Fall, for which I summoned the faithful Louis, who led the way down the long slope in front of the hotel, which was an easy descent, and we strode ahead rapidly. Nor did we need to stay our steps in going to the Upper Fall. So far it was plain sailing, or plain walking; but as we turned to the Lower and greater Fall, the descent was steeper, and it was prudent, if not necessary, to take more cautious steps. Old Louis understood the business better than I, and checked my youthful impetuosity. "Don't be quite so fast, Doctor!" he said; "you'd better go slow. Don't go a-trottin'! If you go a-trottin', you'll get weak in the knees, and can't stop yourself, and the first you know down you'll go! And another thing, don't take short, quick steps, like a woman, but put your foot out well in front, so as to lean your whole weight upon it, and then you'll stand firm." This was a timely caution, and by following it I got down safely, and, standing on the little parapet that is on the very edge of the rushing waters, looked over into the depth below, into which the river makes its plunge of three hundred and sixty feet!

Returning from the falls, I set my face again towards Inspiration Point, keeping Louis for my only companion and guide. Being by ourselves, we jogged slowly through the woods, stopping wherever anything tempted our eyes. There are many grand views along the cliffs. The Lookout has one advantage over Inspiration Point itself in being lower and projecting farther, so that it gives one a nearer view of the Cañon. It is also easier of approach. The path is one that has no terrors, and I almost ran or danced up to the top. This would be the favorite outlook for sightseers, were not their imaginations excited by the prospect of mounting to a point much nearer heaven!

To that at last we came. I had prepared myself by "girding up my loins" with the belt with which I had clambered up the rocks of Gibraltar. Fortunately there was nobody at the Point except a young German, who was travelling in this country, and carried his kodak everywhere, with which he had just taken a snap shot at the head of old "Inspiration." As he had been trained in the army, he was all muscle and no nerves, and feared

THE FALLS OF THE YELLOWSTONE.

not to go anywhere; and the gallant soldier now offered me his strong arm. Thus attended by two valiant men-at-arms, I strode forward like a conqueror and planted my foot on the topmost pinnacle, like Balboa "upon a peak in Darien!" I cannot boast that I exercised any great freedom in my movements, for old Louis held on to me like a bloodhound, and my German friend stood like a lieutenant by the side of his commander! With such supports, the "commander" could not show the white feather, and he not only went to the very tip-end of the Point, but straightened himself up, as if he were Julius Cæsar!

And how far up in the world was he? A thousand feet! As high as the top of the Eiffel Tower, on which he once stood. But there he was protected by a balustrade of iron, against which he could lean in safety. Here there was absolutely nothing—not a rail, nor even a rope to catch hold of in case of giddiness—nothing but the air and the sky!

But there is a fascination even in terror; and having done it once I sprang up eagerly to do it again, and stepping forward, raised myself up to my full height, and even stood on tiptoe for one last look, that should take in the length and depth of the tremendous gulf that yawned beneath.

And now, being somewhat composed in mind, I sit down on the rocks to study a little more in detail the features of this Cañon of the Yellowstone. If I were a man of science, my first thought would be to take its proportions; to measure it—the depth and the length and the breadth of it—to see how deep-laid are its foundations, and how high its battlements—and to study the forces in nature that could make such a rent in the solid globe. The mountains have not been cleft in twain, as in some wild Alpine gorges, by a convulsion of nature, that has torn the earth asunder; nor has the bottom dropped out by a sinking of the crust of the earth, a catastrophe which is supposed by many scientific authorities to have caused the great depression of the Valley of the Yosemite. The cañon is not the work of the earthquake or the volcano. It has not been wrought by fire, but by water, the softest and the gentlest of the elements, instead of the fiercest and the most destructive. "Water wears away stones," but it must have a long time to do it. A few inches would take the span of a human life. Geologists have attempted to compute the time required for Niagara to work its way back from Lake Ontario, the rapids wearing down the cliffs for seven miles, and furrowing a channel two hundred feet deep,

> "Notching the centuries in the eternal rocks."

But the beginning of the recession of Niagara (though it may antedate the existence of man upon the earth) is but of yesterday compared with that of the Yellowstone, which, rippling softly over the rocks, has cut through the solid strata for twenty miles to a depth of five times that of Niagara! Here all calculations fail. The life of man, which is, for us, the unit of time, dwindles to the vanishing point, as we look up to the hoary summits, whose age is reverently compared with that of Him whose "going forth is of old, even from everlasting."

Sitting here in perfect stillness, save the faint murmur of the river far below, the association took me back to another height, on which I stood twelve years since— Mount Sinai. There the impression of awe was far greater than here, but it was relieved by something that is not here. There was the mountain that was once wrapped in cloud, from which issued thunderings and lightnings. But the terror was relieved by a Presence in the cloud, and a Voice that, while it pronounced the inexorable Law, yet coupled with it the word of promise and of hope.

But here all this is wanting. The mountains are stern and silent. The rocks are hard and cold. In the midst of the destructive forces of nature, how lonely is man! He is the most helpless of all creatures. Yonder eagle, sitting on his nest half way down the Cañon, can take care of himself. But man gropes about as one uncared for, and unrecognizing nature crushes him like a worm. With instincts that crave communion, he finds nothing around that gives him even a sign of intelligence. He is in the midst of blind forces, whose only mission is to destroy. In these awful solitudes there is nothing that speaks to him of life, but only of death, inevitable and universal. The sunken Cañon, when darkened by the shadow of the cliffs, or when the clouds hang low above it, seems to be covered with a funeral pall, as if it were a rock-hewn sepulchre, the sepulchre of the world. Such is the awfulness of nature without life and without God!

But while we are " shivering on the brink," the clouds break, and instantly there is a revelation of what was hidden by the darkness. The river, in digging its way through countless ages down into the heart of the earth, has uncovered the strata one after another, till the veins of rock are like veins of blood, streaked upon the old walls, which instantly flash with such brilliancy of color that the whole Cañon is lighted up with ineffable splendor. It is for the moment as if the veil were drawn aside; as if the gates were opened; and we saw things invisible to the natural eye. This is no longer a sepulchre for the dead; it is filled with life, with whispering voices and fluttering wings. There is something more than beauty; there has come into the face of nature an expression of tenderness, the tenderness of God, in whose presence we are no longer trembling and afraid; we are in our Father's house, in the hand not only of infinite power, but of infinite love.

This is not a description of the Cañon of the Yellowstone. I do not attempt to describe the indescribable. But it is better than drawing pictures, to draw from nature itself an inspiration of something that is above nature, a faith that shall be "the light of all our seeing" in this world of shadows.

www.ingramcontent.com/pod-product-compliance
Lightning Source LLC
Chambersburg PA
CBHW031941230426
43672CB00010B/2009